COAST GUIDE

Seabrook, New Hampshire to Freeport, Maine

by Ed and Roon Frost

Scenic Routes by car, bike, and foot
for travelers and natives with information
on beaches, boat trips, historic sites,
shopping, restaurants, nature areas,
attractions for children

Glove Compartment Books
P.O. Box 1602
Portsmouth, New Hampshire

Cover artist is Don Demers, an award-winning illustrator, whose work has appeared in YANKEE MAGAZINE, READERS DIGEST, SAIL MAGAZINE, and DOWN EAST.

Cover design is by Francesca Mastrangelo, who operates Angel Graphic Design Studio, Portsmouth, NH. Her design work includes many regional magazines, such as NEW HAMPSHIRE PROFILES and SEACOAST LIFE.

Maps are by Alex Wallach, a Maine cartographer with a masters degree in geography from the University of Vermont. Formerly with READERS DIGEST (Canada), he has produced maps for several guidebooks to New England and the Mid-Atlantic region.

Layout design and some of the illustrations are the work of Steve Killam, a self-taught commercial artist, whose credits include YANKEE and DOWN EAST Magazines, as well as numerous commercial and industry publications throughout the New England area.

Christine Davidson, who runs Wordswright Editorial Services in Portsmouth, NH, edited COAST GUIDE. The author of STAYING HOME INSTEAD, she has written numerous articles for various seacoast media.

Printing is by Knowlton & McLeary Co., Farmington, ME.

First Edition

ISBN 0-9618806-0-0

From Seabrook to Freeport.

In the beginning it was all one land — from the sand dunes of New Hampshire to Maine's Casco Bay. The same tribe of Indians roamed the whole region. And the original British land grant included everything from what is now Seabrook to Freeport.

Even after the coast was divided up, it was governed by the same authority. For many years the older colony of Massachusetts exerted its influence over northeastern New England, establishing the same standards for everything from schools and roads to behavior in taverns. In times of trouble, settlers in Maine and New Hampshire joined together to meet a common enemy — whether it was the Indians, the French, or eventually their own British governors.

New Hampshire became one of the original thirteen states following the Revolution, while Maine had to wait another forty-five years to separate from Massachusetts. Centuries of different governments have made their mark; still, the people along the coast continue to have much in common, whether it's the way they build a house or dig for clams.

Low tide smells like low tide at Odiorne Point or Wells Beach, and the sunsets can be equally spectacular in either spot. Year after year, tourists flock to this 80-mile stretch of rock and sand for the same cool air, the same historic ambience, the same easygoing pace.

Yet until now, no travel guide has dealt with this region as a whole. Books on New England treat New Hampshire and Maine separately, even along this part of the coast where they were once one. Fortunately, travelers today — like the Europeans and Indians before them — recognize the special qualities that make this coast unique.

How to Use COAST GUIDE.

If you are driving north (most visitors are), start at the beginning of the book, which describes the scenic route, running south to north along the coast. For travelers coming from the north or west, this route can be picked up at any point from Seabrook to Freeport. Italics indicate directions and practical information, like admission fees and facilities; suggested destinations are printed in boldface to help you find them quickly.

Nearby points of interest inland are treated in a separate chapter. Coastal sidetrips, noted by a different typeface, are incorporated into the scenic route whenever possible. Both the inland routes and sidetrips are excellent choices for rainy days or simply a change of landscape.

Throughout COAST GUIDE, we've selected the prettiest routes to take — those that best represent the essence of this part of New England. (Occasionally we'll suggest shortcuts for those who may be in a hurry.) Because rte. 1 is usually congested, we avoid it unless we have a specific destination in mind. Signs refer to it as the "Coastal Route," though you get just one glimpse of the ocean on the highway from Seabrook to Freeport!

Whether you're looking for bargains in sportswear or a good spot to picnic, you'll find them listed en route or in sidetrips — just look for the appropriate symbol in the left-hand margin. Both the scenic route and the side-trips are supplemented with information in the text and pictographs:

BEACH
BICYCLE ROUTE
CHILDREN
CRUISE
EXPENSIVE
FORT
GARDEN
HISTORIC SITE BUILDING OR MUSEUM
INEXPENSIVE
PICNIC FACILITIES
RESTAURANT
SHOPPING
WALKING TOUR OR PATH
WILDLIFE AREA

Background material and pertinent facts about the region will also be highlighted. Finally, we have included numerous maps to help you find your way anywhere along the coast.

COAST GUIDE is just that — neither an encyclopedia nor a press release. We've been thorough in our research, but we've also selected what we, personally, find most appealing here — something publications funded by municipalities or advertisers cannot do. We've tried to give you, as we do our own friends and house-guests, what you need to explore the coast, without spoiling your own sense of discovery.

The idea is for anyone and everyone — day-trippers, summer residents, and people who've lived here all their lives — to have enough information to enjoy this very special part of New England as completely as possible. We hope COAST GUIDE will make your experience here as pleasurable as our own has been.

Ed and Roon Frost
May 1987

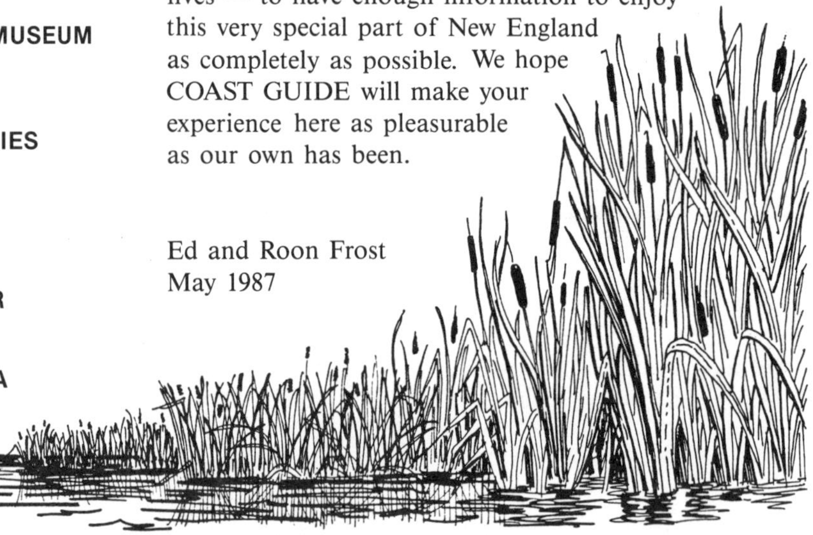

The Scenic Route.

A microcosm of New England, the coast of New Hampshire and southern Maine offers a variety of sights and experiences. A factory outlet sign competes with a rustic barn for your attention. You will drive past fir trees and birches that seem to grow out of rock only to come upon bogs or marshes, full of cattails and sea oats. There's something here for everyone — it's just a matter of knowing where to look.

If you are coming from the south, Exit 2 of the New Hampshire Turnpike is the best place to begin your exploration of the coast. The trip from Boston to Hampton may take less time than you expected — at least once you're out of the city. Unless of course you have chosen to travel on a summer Saturday morning when I-95 North can be jammed. By hitting the traffic right, you can be in this part of New Hampshire in about forty-five minutes from the Tobin Bridge in Boston. *From Exit 2, head east on rte. 51 to 101C.*

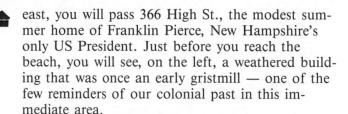

This road, which becomes High Street, leads through what was one of the richest settlements in this area. Good farm land and a protected harbor brought prosperity here in the 17th and 18th centuries. (For further exploration of the Hampton area, see Sidetrips, page 3.) In about ten minutes' drive through what is now a residential area, you'll be able to see the ocean, with nothing but salt water separating you from France. As you continue east, you will pass 366 High St., the modest summer home of Franklin Pierce, New Hampshire's only US President. Just before you reach the beach, you will see, on the left, a weathered building that was once an early gristmill — one of the few reminders of our colonial past in this immediate area.

Hampton was not always on its feet financially. Ex-President Franklin Pierce lent the town $1,500 to help it get through the Civil War period. Prosperity returned with the advent of the trolley from Boston in 1897 and the upgrading of rte. 1A in 1907, bringing tourists to the beach via motorcar.

When you hit rte. 1A, you've arrived at the northern end of the commercial section of ***Hampton Beach***. Rte. 1A runs north and south, following New Hampshire's eighteen-mile coastline. You can go either way, depending on your tastes.

Choices, Choices, Choices.

If you are interested in motels, carryouts, arcades, and lots of exposed skin, head south. Hampton Beach has been called the world's largest ashtray. There are probably more bronzed bodies per square inch on this five-mile stretch of sand than anywhere else north of Atlantic City. But for those who hope to find some space between beach blankets, we recommend moving on north. (Simply skip the coastal sidetrips that follow.)

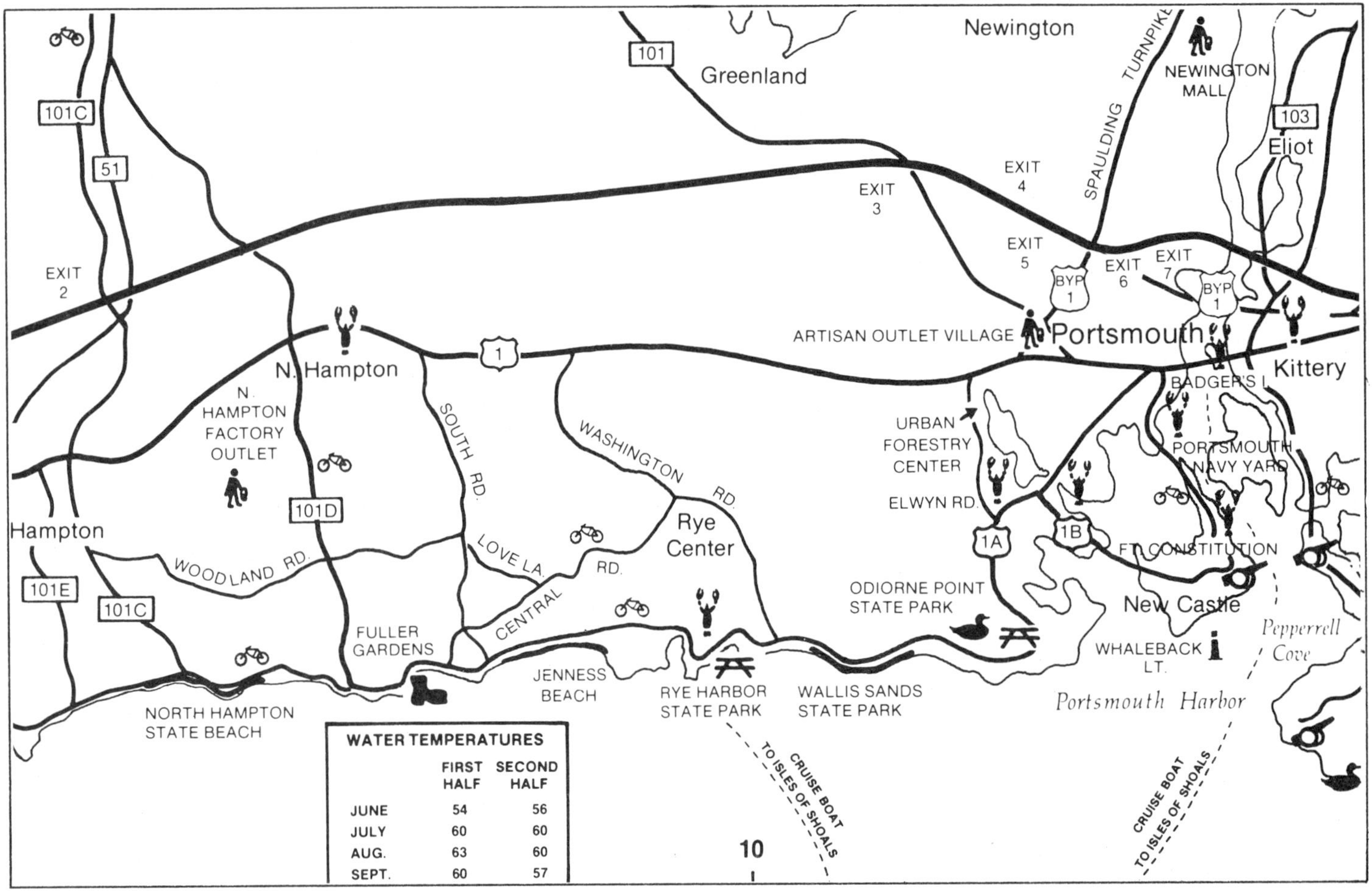

WATER TEMPERATURES

	FIRST HALF	SECOND HALF
JUNE	54	56
JULY	60	60
AUG.	63	60
SEPT.	60	57

Sidetrip: ***Hampton Beach.*** There are plenty of other attractions to the south, once you get through the congestion of beach traffic on Ocean Boulevard (rte. 1A). Unfortunately, bumper-to-bumper cars, pedestrians, and one-way streets can slow you down to a city pace.

If you're looking for nightlife, this is the place to be. Any local newspaper, many of which are free, will list weekly happenings. Choose between:

- **The Hampton Beach Sea Shell** on Ocean Boulevard offers a series of free summer concerts with jazz, popular, and big band sounds.
- **Hampton Beach Casino**, 603/926-4300, just across the street, features top names every night from Judy Collins to rock's latest star.
- **Hampton Playhouse**, rte. 101E, 357 Winnacunnet Road, 603/926-3073, offers good summer-stock productions.

For a quieter time, ***Hampton Harbor Marsh***, the largest salt marsh in New England, has 8,000 acres of mudflats, sea grass, sand bars, and the best clam beds in the northeast. For the naturalist, the ideal time to visit is shortly after Labor Day, when shorebirds outnumber people. The best vantage point is from Hampton Harbor Inlet, just south of the bridge, at low tide.

AMERICAN BITTERN

HAY STADDLE

In colonial times marshland east of what is now rte. 1A was reserved for the use of fishermen, while the marshland to the west was given to farmers, who used the salt hay to feed their cattle. In the fall they cut and stacked the hay on staddles to dry, retrieving it in the spring by boat, or in the winter by horse and sleigh after the water had frozen. Staddles can still be seen here today.

On the west bank of the Blackwater River you can see what put ***Seabrook*** on the map: the $4 billion Nuclear Power Station. Whether or not it is operating by the time you read this will depend on the outcome of the escalating battle between the pros and the antis. It's likely that the Seabrook Station Education Center, 603/474-9521, on rte. 1, will be open, even if the power plant is not. *Free; open Tuesdays-Fridays 1-4 pm. Bus tours at 2:30 pm; environmental trail through the marsh.*

Originally part of Hampton, this small community also has a lesser-known claim to fame: Al Capp based "Dog Patch" in his L'il Abner cartoon on Seabrook. The town has always been physically isolated from the surrounding area, so when Capp, who lived in nearby

Hampton Falls, conceived the idea for his strip, he used this coastal community as a model for Daisy Mae's home.

Some Beaches For Relaxing.

The drive on rte. 1A north of the commercial section of Hampton Beach offers a relaxed pace. Before long you will see some of the most appealing scenery along the coast. From this part of the road you rarely lose sight of the crashing surf, and there are plenty of spots to pull over, stretch your legs, and fill your lungs with clean salt air.

There's even a good restaurant: RON'S BEACH HOUSE, 965 Ocean Blvd., 603/926-1870, on your left at Plaice Cove. A modest, white-washed beach house, Ron's serves a casual lunch upstairs and dinner below in a pleasant dining room. Smoked coho salmon, native crab soup with an oriental flavor, lobster croissant, sole Orly, veal "au poivre," and an appealing raw bar make this a popular place to stop.

If you are ready to take the plunge, proceed north along rte. 1A to ***North Hampton State Beach***. *Metered parking, rest rooms, changing area, but no picnic facilities. (Not to worry, we have a special picnic spot in mind up ahead at Rye Harbor.)* If you'd rather walk than sun or swim, there's a two-mile path that winds along the coast over the promontory known as Little Boars Head all the way to the Rye Beach Club. It has marvelous views — not only of the Atlantic crashing onto the shore but also of the generously-spaced, opulent "cottages" (a classic example of New England understatement), also known as Millionaire's Row.

When you reach Atlantic Avenue (rte. 101D), look for signs to ***Fuller Gardens***, once part of the estate of former Massachusetts Governor Alvan Fuller. Two acres of formal gardens here are open to the public. Of special interest are the roses — 1500 in all —

and the Japanese garden. *Admission, open daily 10-6 early May through through mid-October. 603/964-5414.* If you find this area to your taste, there are scenic drives or bike trips you might enjoy as well.

Many New England colonial settlements were protected by guns; this part of the coast was protected by a rock. Indian legend describes this region as taboo, referring to a white god buried under a rock. Near Little Boars Head a rock exists with markings believed to have been made by Norsemen. It is said that the explorer Thorvald was killed by Indians in 1003, and the rock marks his grave. This may explain why there were fewer Indian attacks here than in neighboring communities.

Sidetrip: ***North Hampton.*** Take Atlantic Avenue (Rt. 101D) west for about two miles. This quiet country road has wide shoulders for biking and passes through some of the prettiest farmland in the area, including a horse farm on the left where the 1968 Kentucky Derby winner Dancer's Image was bred. A large sign makes it difficult to miss. The town of North Hampton itself consists of little more than a town hall, fire station, and delicatessen, but the scenery on the way makes the trip worthwhile.

Rye.

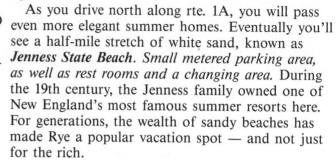

As you drive north along rte. 1A, you will pass even more elegant summer homes. Eventually you'll see a half-mile stretch of white sand, known as ***Jenness State Beach***. *Small metered parking area, as well as rest rooms and a changing area.* During the 19th century, the Jenness family owned one of New England's most famous summer resorts here. For generations, the wealth of sandy beaches has made Rye a popular vacation spot — and not just for the rich.

"As a summer resort [Rye] has a social atmosphere differing widely from that prevailing at either Newport or Coney Island; neither fashions nor fakers rule supreme. It is essentially a resting place for those wearied with the ceaseless whirl of society or the cares of business." Local historian Langdon B. Parsons, 1905.

Sidetrip: ***Rye Center.*** Turn left onto Sea Rd., just before Jenness Beach. This will end at Central Rd.; turn right, and after two miles of pretty landscape, you will arrive at the charming village. Turn right onto Washington St., and follow it back to rte. 1A, just north of Rye Harbor.

Further along rte. 1A is ***Rye Harbor***, a small, granite-bound inlet usually full of picturesque fishing boats. Although busy and crowded, this tight little hole in the beach can be a welcome shelter to sailors (the entrance is clearly marked on charts). ***New Hampshire Sea Coast Cruises***, 603/964-5545, offers Isles of Shoals and lobstering trips from the harbor, or can run you up to Portsmouth by water. *Fee; operates May — mid-October. Refreshments and facilities on board. Whale-watching three days a week in season.*

Traditionally, lobstermen made their own traps in the winter from thin slats of oak and ash; the latter was preferred since it was less susceptible to worms. Most were unpainted and weighted down with rocks. It was years before lobstermen gave up their tarred hemp bait bags for nylon ones, and only recently have the locals switched to metal traps.

There are restaurants nearby with splendid views: SAUNDER'S AT RYE HARBOR, 603/964-6466, has a deck for casual dining, while THE PILOT HOUSE RESTAURANT, 603/964-8080, serves up live jazz with dinner. Just beyond on a rocky point overlooking the harbor is ***Rye Harbor State Park*** where you can see the Isles of Shoals, first charted by Captain John Smith in 1614. This spit of land is the place we had in mind for picnicking. *Admission, rest rooms, grills, and picnic tables.*

The next sandy spot may be the best of New Hampshire's public beaches: ***Wallis Sands***. While only 800 feet long, it is 150 feet wide at high tide. Just north of the beach are rocks where harbor seals sometimes sun themselves. *Admission includes parking in a large lot close to the beach and a bathhouse with showers; refreshment stand nearby.*

More Than Just Another Beach.

Further north you will come to a state park that holds appeal for everyone: ***Odiorne Point State Park***. This 230-acre park has a long history. It was originally a trading post in the seventeenth century and later became the first permanent English settlement in New Hampshire. For the next three hundred years it was held privately by the Odiorne family. In 1869 the Sagamore Hotel, an elegant resort opened, only to burn down two years later.

After the bombing of Pearl Harbor, the U.S. Army commandeered the elegant mansions and gardens, turning the property into a base to protect Portsmouth harbor from enemy submarines. Later it became a radar site for the Air Force and National Guard. Now all that remains of the base are the dirt-covered bunkers and concrete casements — great fun for kids. Several miles of trails, some paved, wind their way through the woods, along the rocky shore, and next to the salt marshes, offering a variety of habitats for wildlife. An im-

KC-135

> **The Military Presence.** Throughout coastal New Hampshire and southern Maine, there is a constant military presence on land, at sea, and in the air. On land there are forts from the American Revolution, French and Indian Wars, and the War of 1812, as well as casements and bunkers from more recent wars. Along the New Hampshire coast, you will occasionally see concrete lookout towers from World War II. Some of them have been converted into unusual houses.
>
> Anywhere in this area at any time of day or night, there is a good chance that a KC-135 Stratotanker (used for refueling jets in midair) or an FB-111A fighter bomber will be taking off or landing at Pease Air Force Base. This major Strategic Air Command facility is the home of the 509th Bombardment Wing, 45th Air Division, and the 157th Air Refueling Group of the New Hampshire National Guard. Because of its two-mile-long runway, Pease has been designated as an emergency landing site for the space shuttle.

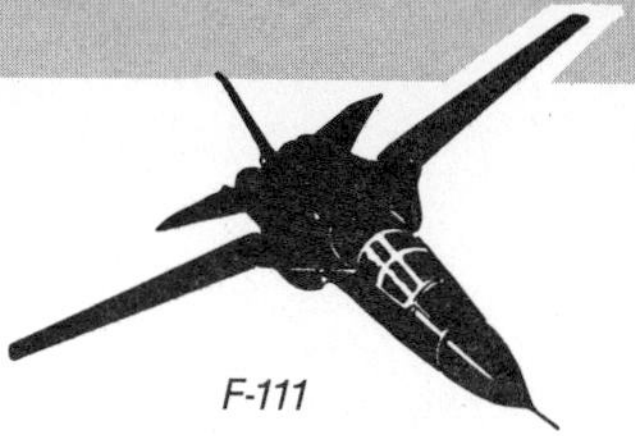

F-111

pressive 194 species of birds have been recorded in the park, as well as 18 species of mammals, and 347 species of plants. *The south end of the park is well-developed, with a large parking area and extensive picnic facilities; small fee. Nature center (free) with "touch tank" of sea creatures; weekend programs on marine life. 603/436-8043. If you are seeking isolation, head north from the parking lot.*

Of interest is the "drowned forest," consisting of 4,000-year-old stumps of pine, birch, and hemlock still rooted to the soil about two feet below the water at low tide. You can see stumps at Stony Pond, an inlet at the south end of the park, if your timing is just right.

Rte. 1A winds north through the salt marshes of Odiorne Point before crossing Seavey's Creek. The road meanders inland for about a mile, through a wooded residential section of Rye. *When you reach rte. 1-B, turn right* toward what was once known as Great Island.

¢ Two inexpensive restaurants to consider:

- THE GOLDEN EGG, 603/436-0519, on 1A, one block beyond 1B, offers superb home-made breakfasts and lunches in attractive surroundings.
- THE ICE HOUSE, 603/431-3086, a rustic eatery in a pine grove on the right side of 1B, is the best place for fried clams or an elaborate sundae.

The road passes through the lush green fairways of the ***Wentworth-by-the-Sea*** Golf Course, 603/431-5930, a well-maintained course, with many holes offering beautiful views of Witch Creek and Little Harbor. Ahead is the impressive resort hotel — one of the largest wood-frame structures in New England. Built in 1874, it was an elegant destination for well-heeled vacationers. More recently the hotel has fallen upon hard times and may still look like something out of a Stephen King novel, as you drive by. However, developers have bought the Wentworth and promise to give this grande dame a face lift, in addition to building condos on the still gracious grounds.

That Famous Ride of Paul Revere: Henry Wadsworth Longfellow immortalized Paul Revere's midnight ride from Boston to Lexington to alert the Minutemen of the impending attack by the British in April of 1775, but his first important ride was from Boston to New Hampshire in January of the same year. His purpose was to alert the citizens of the seacoast that British troops were coming from Boston to reinforce Fort William and Mary in New Castle (now Fort Constitution). The locals quickly captured the fort, took nearly 100 barrels of gunpowder, putting them on their gundalows, and sailed them upriver, where they were hidden until they were needed for the Battle of Bunker Hill. Many barrels were stored in private homes in Exeter.

Rte. 1B continues north through a sparsely settled part of New Castle, passing ***Great Island Common***, a pretty little beach with wonderful views of lighthouses and an abandoned Coast Guard station. *Small fee; grills and picnic facilities, rest rooms, games areas, playgound.* Next you will come to the quaint colonial village of ***New Castle***. On your right you'll see signs for ***Fort Constitution Historic Site***, worth visiting, as it may be the only fort in America which garrisoned soldiers in every national conflict from the Revolution to World War II. When you're done, you may want to amble around the narrow streets of the village.

For over two hundred years, New Castle was a prosperous fishing community which could be reached only by boat; the streets evolved from footpaths, as horses and carriages remained on the mainland. Don't let the numbers on the homes here confuse you — 1647, 1760, 1660, 1800, 1725 are not street numbers but rather the years these houses were built. Today, the village is the kind of place where homes rarely, if ever, make it to the commercial real estate market; the combination of historic charm and water views means that most houses here are sold by word-of-mouth.

Rte. 1B winds slowly through New Castle before going down a hill past a cemetery toward Sagamore Creek. From the two bridges that you cross, you have serene water views in all directions. Among the uninhabited islands on the left is Pest Island, once an isolation center for smallpox victims during epidemics.

On the right, across the Piscataqua River (pronounced Pis-ca-ta-qua), is the Portsmouth Naval Prison. During the Spanish American War, it was a tent colony for prisoners. From 1905-1974, when it was boarded up, it housed nearly 83,000 inmates.

Rte. 1B also gives a good view of the Portsmouth Naval Shipyard, where ships of the American fleet have been built or overhauled since 1798 when Benjamin Stoddard, the Secretary of the Navy, bought 58-acre Fernald's Island for $5500. This road will also take you into one of New England's finest ports — a fascinating city to visit.

*In **Portsmouth,** follow rte. 1B to Marcy St., which bears to the right after the Blue Fin Fish Market. This narrow street will take you through an old part of town and past Strawbery Banke, a charming restoration of the original settlement. If you plan to visit the shops and homes in the Banke you can park in their lot on the left. (For more on this historic area, see pages 13-14).*

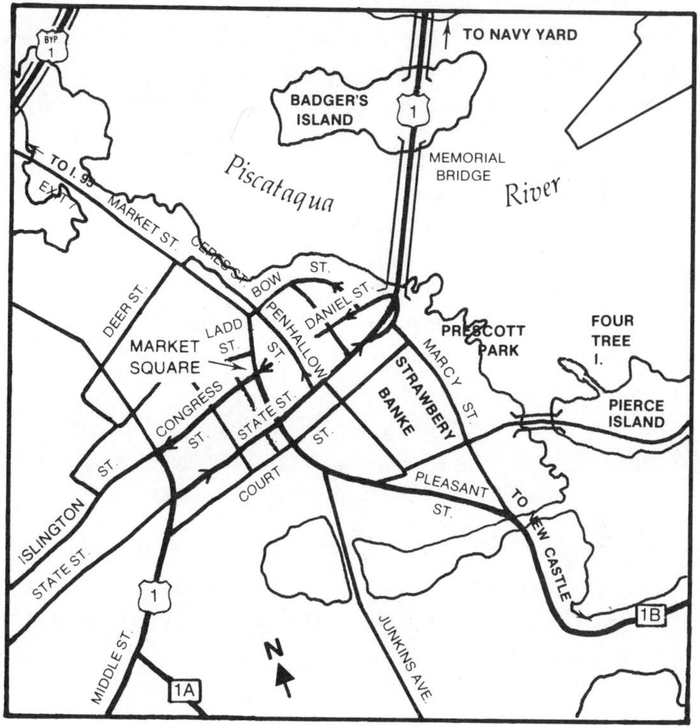

DOWNTOWN PORTSMOUTH

Otherwise, continue past Prescott Park on your right to the end of Marcy St. and head right, under the bridge to the parking garage at Harbour Place on the other side. If that lot is full, continue up the hill to the stop sign. Turn right onto Bow St. to its end at Market St. Turn right, then take an immediate left onto Hanover St., and the municipal garage will be on your left.

Portsmouth can also be reached quickly from I-95 in just an hour from Boston or Portland. Most of the shops, restaurants, and historic sites are accessible from Exit 7, Market St. Hanover St. will be on the right after you pass the first block of stores. You will see the garage ahead on the left.

Portsmouth.

Whether you're interested in shopping, gourmet dining, or simply yearning for the hustle-bustle of a city again, this working port has much to offer. You may see sailors in foreign uniforms dining in the wharf area or a huge tanker docked next to the road. At this writing Sheraton is building a much-needed hotel in the old port; historic buildings are its neighbors.

A mixture of appealing architectural styles from colonial to contemporary, combined with the intense activity of a genuine port, make Portsmouth real. After all, commerce not only keeps historic towns from becoming too precious, but also breathes life into them. And alive Portsmouth is— with over one hundred restaurants; Market Square's craft shops, fashionable boutiques and art galleries open year-round; the beautifully-restored Strawbery Banke historic area; and Prescott Park with its free concerts in the summer, flower gardens exploding with color, and street vendors selling everything from Scottish scones to charcoal-broiled steaks.

In 1762 the stage chaise for Portsmouth departed Boston at 11 in the morning, arriving at 2 in the afternoon — ***two days later!***

"It's a city . . . but a special New England coastal city, with more than a touch of small-town charm and cooling breezes wafting across the ocean." Glamour Magazine, 1987.

Before the American Revolution, Portsmouth was the largest town in New Hampshire and one of the wealthiest in the colonies. There is still plenty of evidence of prosperity — past and present. But like so many coastal towns, New Hampshire's only seaport has had its ups and downs.

During the last quarter of the 18th century, Portsmouth exported millions of feet of lumber to Great Britain and was turning out fifty vessels a year from its shipyards. Then came Thomas Jefferson's embargo on all foreign trade in 1807, bringing the shipping trade and Portsmouth's fortunes to a standstill. When the embargo was lifted, the shipbuilding industry resumed until the middle of the 19th century. The advent of railroads and steamships put a halt to it permanently. Small local industries took over, particularly breweries, sugar refineries, button factories, and the like. Eventually these businesses disappeared too, but many of the old buildings have been recycled into artist's studios and offices for service industries.

The most visible evidence of economic health today may be seen along the Piscataqua River: big clouds of steam spewing from every opening of a factory that makes drywall; enormous piles of rusting scrap iron destined for far-away lands; and a Matterhorn of road salt to help northern New England get through the winter. In New York City it used to be "Meet me under the clock at the Biltmore"; in Portsmouth it's "Meet me next to the salt pile."

The salt you see is imported from many countries, huge freighters bring it into Portsmouth Harbor where it is stockpiled until needed in the winter to melt snow and ice from area roads. The rusting metal comes from this country — shredded automobiles and appliances delivered from processing plants in Madbury, NH, and Tewksbury, MA — then is shipped to Turkey, India, Greece, Taiwan, Japan, Korea, and Spain where scrap metal still has value.

What to see in Portsmouth:

You won't need a car to see the most interesting parts of Portsmouth. Just park where you can (the best bet is the municipal garage on Hanover St.), amble, and enjoy, keeping in mind that much has happened since the first settlers picked strawberries on the banks of the Piscataqua.

You can start your explorations by taking the ***Portsmouth Trail.*** *From the municipal garage, walk north to Market St. or east to Congress St. Simply follow the red line on the pavement, which connects six important houses in the historic district. You can buy tickets to visit individual houses or a strip ticket that allows entry into all the houses. But be advised that not all the homes are open every day. Also it's possible to spend an entire day on the trail, if you make stops in shops and restaurants en route. Tickets can be purchased at* *the homes themselves or at the Chamber of Commerce office, Market Street Ext., 603/436-1118.*

Moffatt-Ladd House, 154 Market St., 603/436-8221. Built in 1763 as a wedding gift by English sea captain John Moffat for his son, this three-storied manor house is situated high above the harbor. Period antiques, a secret passageway that once led to the wharves, extra deep fireplaces with space for closets on either side, handsome paneling make this an interesting house to visit. Out back are raised flower beds — a "sweet and retired spot" created by owner Alexander Ladd — and the 1823 counting house where Moffatt and Ladd cargoes were laded.

You might want to window-shop a bit along Market or Bow Sts. as you wander through the historic district. And be sure to sample the many restaurants and cafes on Ceres St. *Cross the steps across Market St. from the Moffatt-Ladd House and take the flower-bedecked steps down to the wharf area.* ANNABELLE'S HANDMADE ICE CREAM, 49 Ceres St., 603/431-1988, serves sandwiches and great desserts. You'll want a cone, at least, while you walk. If you're ready for lunch, try TRUE BLUE CAFE overlooking the water, 603/431-6700, for a sophisticated menu that includes local seafood, or FERRY LANDING, 603/431-5510, next door for more traditional fare, like lobster rolls or chili burgers. Both are lively places that allow tourists and locals to rub elbows, while watching tugs and sailboats in the harbor.

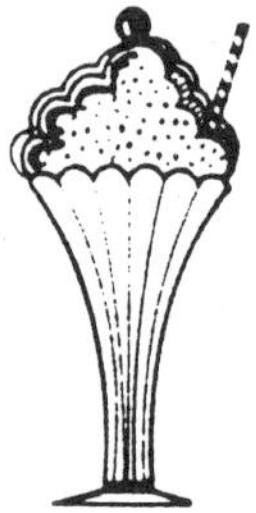

You won't find any floorboards over 23 inches wide in colonial homes here. When New England was a colony, the British reserved the best pine trees for the Royal Navy's ship masts, including the straightest, tallest, and widest trees. All trees of two feet or more in width were marked with the King's "broad arrow," meaning they were not to be used for the colonists' home construction. This was one more irritation that eventually led to the American Revolution.

General William Whipple, who married Catherine Moffatt, lived here for many years. A ship captain in the triangle trade, Whipple imported slaves and owned several himself. The Revolution made him sensitive to the value of individual rights, however, and Whipple decided to free his personal servant, Prince, who later became a respected Portsmouth citizen.

From Ceres St., walk up Bow to Chapel St., noting the vaults built up high in the wall at St. John's Church. Paul Revere recast the church's bell, which colonials had brought home as a prize from Nova Scotia in 1745, after Portsmouth's 1806 fire damaged it. The last house on your left is:

• ***Warner House***, 150 Daniel St., 603/436-5909. Possibly the finest brick city mansion of the colonial period in New England, this home cost £6000 to build from Dutch bricks — the walls are a massive 18 inches thick. Murals were uncovered when old wallpaper was removed in a 19th century restoration, and Benjamin Franklin is said to have installed a lightning rod here in 1762.

• ***Wentworth-Gardner House***, Mechanic St., 603/436-4406. Extensively restored, this may be the best example of Georgian architecture in America. Interior carvings took 14 months to complete. The kitchen fireplace has a windmill spit; original Dutch tiles ornament hearths here.

• ***Gov. John Langdon House***, 143 Pleasant St., 603/431-1800. George Washington not only slept here; he called this prosperous merchant's home "the finest" in Portsmouth. Family antiques, a large rear wing added by Stanford White in the Colonial Revival style, and carefully landscaped grounds make it still one of the city's grandest homes.

• ***Rundlett-May House***, 364 Middle St. (between Summer St. and Miller Ave.), 603/431-1800. This superb Federal-style house has seen little structural change since it was built in 1807. Even the courtyard and garden are in keeping with the original design.

• ***John Paul Jones House***, Middle and State Sts., 603/436-8420, may look familiar — a TV commercial for Sears latex paint made this home famous in the 1970s. Widow Sarah Wentworth Purcell rented Naval hero John Paul Jones a place to hang his hat, while overseeing construction of ships for the Continental Navy. Today this attractive gambrel is home to the Portsmouth Historical Society, who will answer your questions about the leather buckets hanging up here or guide you through their collections of costumes, glass, ceramics, guns, silver, canes, and 18th century documents.

History Out in the Open

The red Portsmouth Trail will also lead you by ***Strawbery Banke***, a ten-acre open-air seaport neighborhood consisting of more than 30 historic buildings (with present-day craftsmen working at the old trades in some of them). Within the Banke area are various architectural styles from the 17th to 20th centuries. The newest restorations include the Drisco House, decorated in two distinct time periods from this home's past: the east end representing the 1790s store and the west side recreating a portion of an apartment from the 1950s. Also of interest is the William Pitt Tavern on Court St., which played an important role in Portsmouth's revolutionary history.

In addition to other restorations — Sherburne House (1695), Chase House (1762), the Captain John Wheelwright House (1780), Thomas Bailey Aldrich House (1790), Captain Keyran Walsh House (1796), and the Governor Goodwin Mansion (1811) — you might consider one of Strawbery Banke's specialized events, including a horticultural tour (Victorian flower garden, antique herbal garden, colonial revival gardens), or an archeaological tour. *For specific information on these and other seasonal events, call 603/433-1100. Admission.*

Just across Marcy Street from Strawbery Banke is ***Prescott Park***, a wonderful source of free entertainment all summer long. The Sheafe Warehouse, where John Paul Jones outfitted the frigate "Ranger," is now a folk art museum with ship models and hand-carved mastheads. The newly-restored brick building on Marcy St. is home to the Portsmouth Heritage Museum with artifacts, paintings, and displays relating to the city. You'll find everything from a gundalow to relics from the U.S.S. Portsmouth.

> "Portsmouth-built ships and New York merchants — the superiority of one is equalled by the enterprise of the other." Toast at a Portsmouth ship launching, 1851.

Nearby flower gardens and shady lawns are a delightful place to relax and sample food or drink from the numerous vendors. In the evenings there are free performances of popular Broadway musicals. (Recently "The Music Man" and "West Side Story" played under the stars here). *Bring your own blankets and a picnic supper. If you're spending much time in the area, you may want to get a current schedule of Prescott Park's Arts Festival exhibits and children's workshops; 603/436-2848.*

Nearby are islands for more outdoor activities. One of our favorites is ***Four Tree Island***. A snowy owl lives here in the winter and seagulls perch on the sculpture, "My Mother The Wind," dedicated "For those who sailed here to find a new life." *Pavilions, grills, rest rooms.* ***Pierce Island***, owned by the city, has one of the few public swimming pools in the area. *Minimal admission; open to the public 1-5 pm, 7 days per week, from the end of June to the end of August; locker room, showers; 603/431-2000, ext. 279.*

Further Explorations.

Not all of Portsmouth's historic homes are on the red trail. The Little Harbor home of Governor Benning Wentworth, who perhaps more than any other royal official helped transform the bustling young port into a provincial capital of grace and style, is some distance from downtown. But this home can be a pleasant drive or bike trip for those with a little time to spare. *Heading north on State St., toward the river, turn right on Pleasant St., then right on Junkins Ave., and right again on South St. By the cemetery (the Proprietor's Burying Ground), turn left at the light. Then look for a sign on your left to Little Harbor Rd. and turn left, passing through a lovely pine woods. The last house on the point is:*

- ***Wentworth-Coolidge Mansion***, Little Harbor Rd., 603/436-6607. This rambling 52-room home is tied together by "unlooked for steps and capricious little passages" from numerous additions. Wentworth's cellar could hold 30 horses in case of an emergency; there are the governor's Council Chambers, a "spy room," card rooms, a billiard room, and views of what remains a quiet anchorage outside Portsmouth harbor. *Fee.*

History buffs may want to find the city's oldest house, located in a work-a-day part of Portsmouth:

- ***The Jackson House***, the central section of which was built around 1664 by an early shipbuilder, has a roof that slopes down nearly to the ground on one side. Weathered clapboards, an unadorned front door, roughly plastered walls, exposed beams, and wide-board floors combine to make a solid, functional home, typical of the early colonial period. *From the municipal garage, head west on Hanover to the first traffic light and turn right onto Maplewood Ave. Cross the bridge and turn right onto Northwest St. The House is one block up the hill on your right. Admission; open by appointment. 603/436-3205.*

History and nature mingle comfortably at the ***Urban Forestry Center***, 45 Elwyn Rd., 603/431-6774, a veritable time-warp in the midst of the suburban sprawl off Lafayette Rd. (rte. 1). Managed by the NH Forests and Lands Division, the Center is privately endowed, a gift of John Elwyn Stone, a descendant of John Langdon. Herb gardens, wildlife trails through the salt marshes, and comfortable restorations prove that the words "city" and "woods" can still be synonymous. *Drive as you would from downtown toward the Wentworth-Coolidge Mansion, but continue past Little Harbor Rd. over the bridge at Sagamore Creek for about a mile to the flashing light at*

Elwyn Rd. Take a sharp right and drive approximately two miles to the entrance to the Urban Foresty Center on the right. For directions from I-95 or rte. 1, see Sidetrips section, page 82.

> Why is a saltmarsh important? Formed from glacial deposits, coastal marshes are fertile ecosystems, fed and cleansed by tidal flows. Marshes provide a natural form of flood control, are home to most commercial shell or sport fish at some point in their development, and offer numerous recreational outlets for us all.

Sightsee Sitting Down.

If you prefer to leave your car in the garage, there are one-hour narrated tours that take visitors through the streets of Portsmouth and across the creek to New Castle on a reproduction trolley. These trips can help to get your bearings quickly. *The tours are offered by* ***Olde Port Trolley Co.****, and depart from Albacore Park on Market St. Ext., Portsmouth Harbor Cruises dock on Ceres St., the Isles of Shoals Cruises dock on Market St., and Strawbery Banke on Marcy St. 603/692-5111. Small fee.*

There are also several excellent cruises available from Portsmouth. Besides whale-watching trips, ***Isles of Shoals Cruises*** offers two-and-a-half-hour round trips out to sea or to the Isles of Shoals, where you can arrange to spend the day picnicking or exploring Star Island (free tour, dining facilities, playground, bookstore on the island). *Food and drink are also served on board. Bathroom facilities. Tickets may need to be purchased in advance in season; fees vary according to cruise. The dock is next to the salt pile on Market St. Ext. 603/431-5500.*

> "Sailing out from Portsmouth Harbor with a fair wind from the northwest, the Isles of Shoals lie straight before you . . . ill-defined and cloudy shapes, faintly discernible in the distance. . . . As you approach they separate, and show each its own peculiar characteristics . . .
>
> "Swept by every wind that blows, and beaten by the bitter brine for unknown ages, well may the Isles of Shoals be barren, bleak, and bare. . . . But to the human creature who has eyes that will see and ears that will hear, nature appeals with such a novel charm, that the luxurious beauty of the [main]land is half forgotten before one is aware." Celia Thaxter, 1873.

Before the first house was built in Portsmouth, 600 fishermen lived on Appledore Island, one of the ***Isles of Shoals***. In colonial days Appledore was part of Maine, then under the jurisdiction of the Massachusetts Bay Colony. When taxed, the fishermen on Appledore simply up and floated over to Star Island, in New Hampshire. During the Revolution, inhabitants of all these islands were ordered back to the mainland. The early days of the new nation saw resettlement there with construction of a ropewalk, windmill, saltworks, bakery, cooper's shop, gristmill, and tavern.

In the mid-19th century, the islands became a fashionable resort. Appledore Hotel was a haven for the friends of poetess Celia Thaxter, who grew up on the Isles of Shoals — John Greenleaf Whittier, James Russell Lowell, Harriet Beecher Stowe, and Childe Hassam all summered here.

Although New Hampshire's coastline is only eighteen miles long, its rivers add close to a hundred miles of shoreline washed by salt water. Of these, the Piscataqua and its tributaries may be the most beautiful and are steeped in as much history as Portsmouth itself. Unfortunately, there are few roads along these waters. And due to the river's swift current and narrow channel from Pierce's Island inland, we recommend that visitors sail these waters only with experienced yachtsmen who know them well.

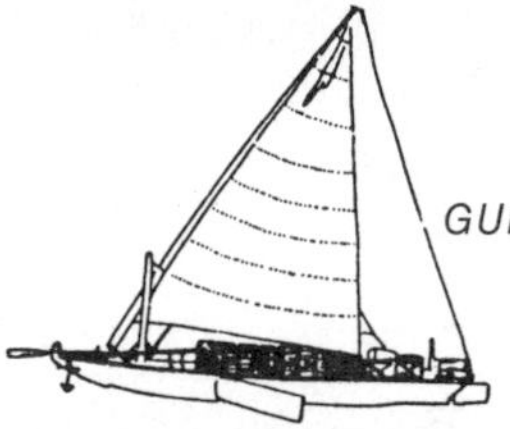

GUNDALOW

If you'd like to explore the Piscataqua, Great Bay, or inland rivers, ***Portsmouth Harbor Cruises*** has several interesting tours available, in addition to its harbor and islands tours. *Narrative, snack bar, and rest room facilities on board. Reservations recommended; admission. Ceres Street, 603/436-8084.*

The main channel to Portsmouth's wharves lies between Pierce's and Seavey's Islands, where it is only 300 to 400 yards wide; the current runs six knots at spring ebb with eight to ten foot tides. Further upriver, sailors look for "horse races" as the white caps between Dover Point and Newington are called, before the river splits into two channels.

The Piscataqua River and Great Bay played as important a role in Portsmouth's sea-faring past as did the city's harbor and islands. There were fishermen and traders near Dover Point when the first settlers arrived at Strawbery Banke. In colonial days shortages of good timber in England, Holland, France and Spain brought a living to lumbermen and shipbuilders of the region. Between 1692 and 1714 some 40 Piscataqua-built ships registered at Boston Customs House. In the 19th century, gundalows — stump-masted, spoon-bowed craft — carried heavy loads along the inland shores. The Piscataqua packet — a prettier, less-rugged keel boat — was a common, if somewhat erratic, means of transportation for residents.

Although parts of the river are heavily industrialized, the shoreline of the 24-square-mile basin that is Great Bay remains pastoral, much the way the early settlers and colonists knew it. When Aristotle Onassis proposed building a huge oil refinery on the bay in 1973, he was roundly beaten by the citizens of the eight towns that front Great Bay. Today, the shallow bay has been seeded with oysters; shorebirds, ducks, and Canada geese flock to its waters.

Upriver by the Sprague Oil Refinery remain the remnants of wooden Ferris Steamers, built by the Shattuck Shipyard in Newington to help carry supplies to the Allies in World War I. Using horse power of the four-legged variety, pneumatic tools and derricks, the shipyard framed a 3,500 ton vessel in three-and-a-half days, breaking a wartime record — thanks to 60 men working round the clock.

Traveling with Children?

While Prescott Park, Strawbery Banke, and many of the other kinds of sightseeing along the seacoast may be as enjoyable for children as adults, there are some very special treats in the area — created just for kids:

- Water Country, rte. 1, Portsmouth 603/436-3556. As commercial amusement parks go, this is a class act. The huge water park has several giant slides, large swimming pools, bumper boats, and refreshments. This may be just the place to spend a warm day with youngsters tired of riding in the car. *Admission. From the Portsmouth Traffic Circle, follow signs to NH beaches to rte. 1, about four miles on the right.*
- The Children's Museum of Portsmouth, Meetinghouse Hill, Marcy St. (rte. 1B), 603/436-3853. *Admission. Handicapped parking at museum, free parking at Pierce Island, off Marcy Street, by Prescott Park. Group rates by prior arrangement; frequent workshops for children and their parents. Museum shop.* Twelve different hands-on exhibits, including the Yellow Submarine, Lobsters and Lobstering, The Clock Tower, computers, arts, and science areas, give children a chance to touch and explore at their own levels of understanding. Parents and teachers will enjoy this museum too!
- The Albacore — Port of Portsmouth Maritime Park, 500 Market St. Ext., 603/436-1331. "The Albacore," made right here in Portsmouth, was one of the most important subs in US history, built as "a full-scale hydrodynamics laboratory." The fastest, quietest, and most maneuverable underwater boat of her day, this submarine is fish shaped with a cod's head and a mackerel's tail. *Admission. 40-minute tours of an actual submarine and museum with films; open daily.*

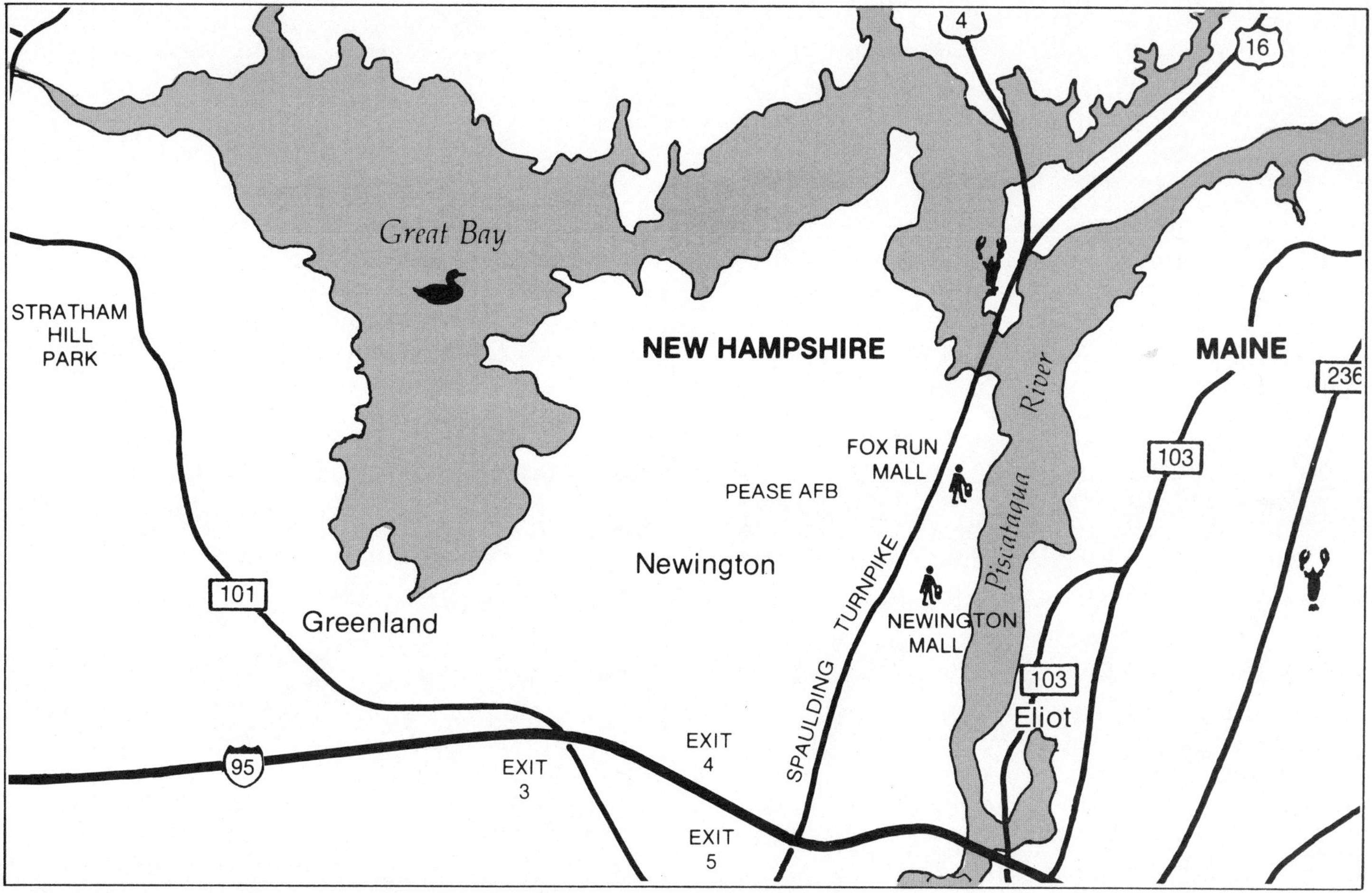
Great Bay
STRATHAM
HILL
PARK
NEW HAMPSHIRE
MAINE
4
16
236
River
Piscataqua
FOX RUN
MALL
PEASE AFB
103
Newington
SPAULDING
TURNPIKE
NEWINGTON
MALL
101
Greenland
103
Eliot
95
EXIT
3
EXIT
4
EXIT
5

Dining Out in Portsmouth.

There are close to a hundred restaurants in this port city of 30,000, ranging from haute cuisine to carry-outs and fast-food franchises. Due to space limitations, we list only our personal favorites, not necessarily the places your motel or bed and breakfast will recommend.

Unquestionably the most famous restaurant in Portsmouth is James Haller's BLUE STRAWBERY, 29 Ceres St., 603/431-6420. Chef Haller, a well-known cookbook author, is innovative with his five-course dinners at the "prix fixe" of $32 per person. There are several choices of entrees and appetizers. Soup, salad, crusty bread with herb butter, three different vegetables, dessert and coffee or tea are served each diner as well.

The kitchen dominates this small restaurant. It's the first thing you see (and smell) on entering. At two seatings each evening, waiters don large white aprons to serve patrons from huge platters. Cookbook ads are a feature on each table, while condiments and ashtrays are not. The wine list is excellent, with many vintages served by the glass. A wonderful creme of palm soup, sharpened with green peppercorns, will arrive in a white crockery mug; plates don't match. But somehow it doesn't matter when you're feasting on things like snails with hot peppers or game hen stuffed with native crab to tempt the palate.

Another fine choice, consistently winning 10s (on a scale of 1 to 10) from a local food critic is STRAWBERY COURT RESTAURANT FRANCAIS, 20 Atkinson St., between State and Court Sts., one block from Prescott Park, 603/431-7722. As intimate as dining in a private home, this restaurant offers a full five-course meal for $35; however, a couple may order a complete dinner for one and just a salad or appetizer and entree for the other, then share. Pheasant pate, cauliflower soup laced with ripe brie, poached salmon with fresh dill, or lobster cooked with saffron are just a few of the specialities — even the bread here is wonderful.

THE GRILL, 37 Bow St., 603/431-6700, is as attractive and non-colonial as any big-city restaurant. The swordfish is as light as a cloud; even the seafood chowder, a staple in this area, is unusual here (the stock is prepared ahead of time with fish, oysters and vegetables added just prior to serving, so they retain their own character). Although these three are all pricey places, The Grill's kitchen also serves the True Blue Cafe (page 12) for more reasonably-priced dining.

In the moderate price range, THE LIBRARY at the Rockingham House, 401 State St., 603/431-5202, attracts a younger crowd, despite its stately appearance. The chef knows his stuff — mussels in white wine, and roast duck are prepared in classic fashion, while other dishes are both novel and delicious.

Just a few feet from the Hanover St. garage, THE METRO, 20 High St., 603/436-0521, is a pleasant, reliable place to dine. Brass, lots of dark wood, and live jazz give a sophistication that many seacoast restaurants lack. Seafood Lorenzo served on artichokes, a classic Caesar salad, steaks and chops are good choices; the wine list includes some interesting and reasonably-priced Australian wines.

ANTHONY'S AL DENTE, 65 Penhallow St., 603/436-2527, is a pleasant surprise, almost hidden away in the grotto-like cellar of an old building between Daniel and State Streets. Pasta is marvelous, as the name suggests, but so are the veal dishes and even the vegetables (crisply fresh and colorful) — a real rarity in most Italian restaurants. The thick stone walls give Anthony's a pleasant old-world ambience, making for cozy winter and cool summer dining.

¢ For breakfast (when you may have to wait), lunch, or dinner, KAREN'S at 105 Daniel St., 603/431-1948, is one of Portsmouth's most popular eateries. If you want a glass of wine with your meal, you must bring your own bottle, but the prices here make it worth the trouble. Vegetarians flock to Karen's for the omelets, spanakopita, and pasta primavera, but the fresh fish, chicken raspberry, Mediterranean shrimp, and London broil are equally well-prepared.

Sunday brunch is the bargain meal at THE TAVERN AT STRAWBERY BANKE, an authentic 18th-century colonial at the corner of Marcy and Court Sts., 603/431-2816. An attractive courtyard, shaded by Norway maples, is the ideal spot for summer dining; eggs benedict or pasta topped with crabmeat are tasty ways to begin the day here.

¢ For more exotic fare, try THE TOUCAN BAR AND GRILL, 174 Fleet St. (across from the municipal garage), 603/431-5443. Chicken salad in a Mexican puff pastry, a tortilla pizza, blackened fish, and popcorn shrimp or crayfish give warm Southern flavor year round here. Kids will love the live toucan; placemats ask to be drawn on (crayons are provided).

> The most expensive item on the menu at the Toucan is also a free plug for the lunch stand across the street: "Two dogs with the works from the guys across the street — $25 (if you want 'em bad enough, we'll get 'em for you.)"

GILLEY'S Wagon, 603/431-6343, in the vacant lot across the street has the best hot dogs around and genuine New England baked beans.

SAKURA JAPANESE RESTAURANT, 40 Pleasant St. just off Market Square, 603/431-2721, is a relative newcomer that's fast packing diners in. A small, simple replica of Japanese restaurants — sushi bar with plain tables and chairs out front, and cushioned boothes in the more private area toward the back — Sakura's food is tasty and fresh, whether you're having miso soup, tempura, an orange cut to be eaten with chopsticks, or bean cake.

CAFE BRIOCHE, 14 Market Square, 603/430-9225, is the best place around for cappuccino, croissants, and people-watching, though the sandwiches, soups and salads make delightful take-out picnics, too.

A MOVEABLE FEAST, 41 Congress St., 603/436-1466, primarily a catering and gourmet food shop, also offers elegant meals to go — an easy way to have a quiet candlelight dinner or for a soup and salad picnic on a pretty day.

If there's one restaurant that tourists flock to, it's YOKEN'S, 603/436-8224, just across from the Urban Forestry Center, on Lafayette Rd. (rte. 1). If you're not put off by the busloads of fellow travelers, this restaurant may be the best buy for your money. No-frills New England cooking and fresh seafood are staples here. On request, your favorite dish will be cooked without salt or saturated fats. The kids will enjoy trying to open the treasure chest in the lobby with the key that accompanies your check; several gift shops.

For night owls we recommend the piano bar at SEVENTY-TWO, 45 Pearl St., 603/436-5666. You must pass through the dining room of this converted church to the choir loft above, but the pianists here are expert enough to make anyone who sings along sound angelic. THE PRESS ROOM, 77 Daniel St., 603/431-5186, has the best in live jazz.

Kittery, Gateway to Maine.

If you are continuing the scenic route from the historic district of Portsmouth, follow rte. 1 over Memorial Bridge into Maine. Of the three bridges that connect Portsmouth to Kittery, Memorial Bridge is the oldest and easternmost. It is also a drawbridge, and assuming you're not in a hurry, you may consider yourself lucky if the bridge is up. Whatever comes through the channel is free entertainment, whether it's just a little sailboat, or a foreign freighter so big that the deckhands are actually looking down at you.

The tide races under Memorial Bridge at seven miles an hour. New England Telephone, not too many years ago, sent underwater divers into the river here to check the phone cable. They reported seeing large boulders rolling along the river floor, like so many marbles.

As you cross over the bridge, look downriver, to your right at the base of the big complex of buildings, and you will likely see the black hull of a nuclear submarine being overhauled at the Portsmouth Naval Shipyard. Since 1917 the Navy Yard has built over 100 submarines; today, more than 7,000 workers help overhaul our fleet of nuclear subs.

When you reach the other side of the drawbridge you will be on Badger's Island, part of ***Kittery, Maine***. Here, over three centuries ago, the sloop-of-war "Ranger" was constructed and sailed for France under the command of John Paul Jones; it was the first government ship to sail under the new American flag. The Badger's Island-built "Typhoon" sailed from Portsmouth to Liverpool in 1851, breaking the record for an Atlantic crossing. Yet another ship constructed here was the sloop-of-war "Kearsarge," which sank the Confederate "Alabama" during the Civil War.

"Redfish," built at the Navy Yard, was the first sub to sail beneath the Arctic ice cap in 1952. Two years later she began a Hollywood career — first in Walt Disney's "Twenty Thousand Leagues Under the Sea," then in "Run Silent, Run Deep." Decorated soldier Audie Murphy starred in the sub's last film, "Battle of Bloody Beach" and may have finally met his match in the "Redfish." "It's all very interesting down there," he said, "but not quite roomy enough for me."

The view back toward Portsmouth harbor from Badger's Island is especially appealing. On warm days the picnic tables at THE CLAM HUT offer the best vantage point to watch boat traffic. Steamed hot dogs and fried clams are popular fare here.

After crossing another little bridge you will be on the mainland. If you're ready for some Maine lobster, boiled with plenty of melted butter, WARREN'S (207/439-1630) on your immediate right is hard to beat. Water views, a huge salad bar, and reasonable prices make this restaurant popular with locals and tourists alike.

Sidetrip: ***Kittery Historical and Naval Museum*** at the junction of rte. 1 north and rte. 236. Bear left for rte. 1, continue for about two miles to the rotary (what New Englanders call traffic circles). Go half way around the circle and look for the museum on your right. Filled with nautical devices and ship models, this small museum is a good place to learn more about Kittery's relationship with the sea. *Open year-round, admission 207/439-3080.*

Sidetrip: **Kittery Factory Outlets**. This mile-long strip of over sixty stores is open daily, whether you want to hunt for bargains or just browse. Osh-Kosh, Black & Decker, Anne Klein, Hathaway Shirts, Towle Silver, and numerous other "name" brands offer discounted merchandise here. *To reach the outlet strip, follow the directions above to the Naval Museum, but stay on rte. 1 for another mile.*

For a glimpse of coastal Maine — in just one town — avoid rte. 1, and stay in the right lane to the stop sign. Then turn right onto Government St., which will take you into downtown Kittery, Maine's oldest incorporated town. This is a down-to-earth business district, serving the Navy Yard and the tiny courthouse. Just consider it a contrast to the upscale boutiquey villages catering to the summer folk, further along the coast. *Be advised to avoid this area on weekday afternoons between 4:00 and 4:30, as that's when the shift changes at the Navy Yard.*

Government St. then turns into rte. 103, which will take you north along the water. As you meander up and down the little hills of the residential part of Kittery, you will see a variety of housing styles, the predominant one being the "New Englander," which we loosely define as any house which is not colonial and would look out of place anywhere but here.

"The summer is slipping away in a perfect delight of weather. Such air as this I never dreamed of. . . . " William Dean Howells' letter to Henry James, July 31, 1898.

Before too many bends in the road you will come to the bridge that spans Spruce Creek. On the north side, colorful lobster buoys bob serenely in the calm waters, while on the south side the boiling currents of the Piscataqua rush out to sea. Watch out for fishermen casting their lines, especially if the car windows are down.

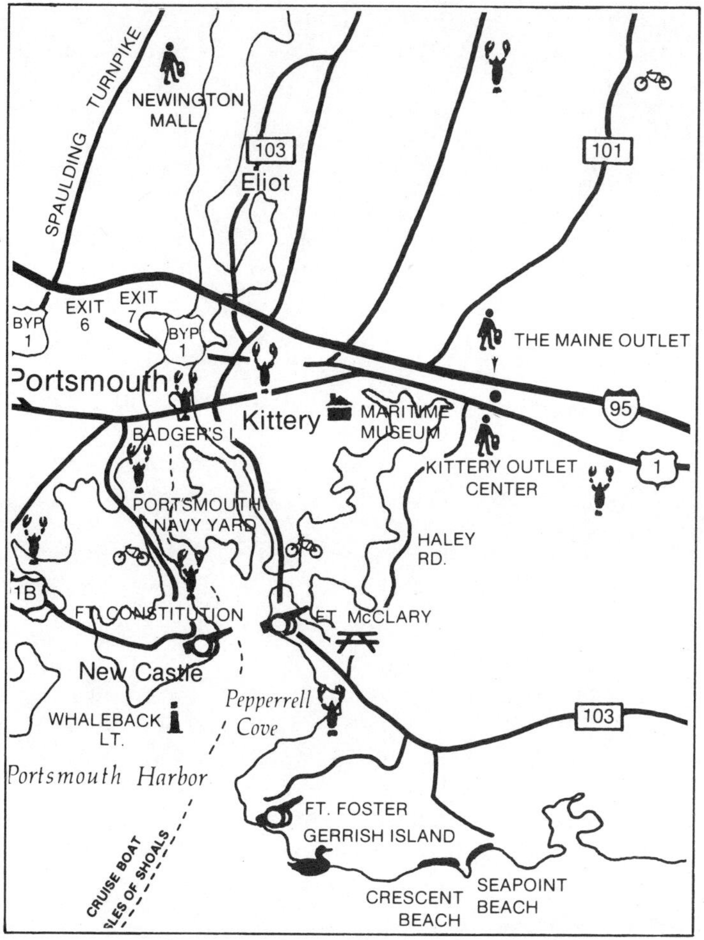

Beyond the bridge is ***Kittery Point*** (same government, different post office). Suddenly the air seems fresher and cooler — surprisingly, it often is. The road takes a couple of sharp turns, passing an elegant Georgian manor house on the right, the Lady Pepperrell House, privately owned.

Before she became Lady Pepperrell, Mary Hirst was orphaned and forced to leave her home in Boston to live with her uncle, a minister in York, ME. There her cousin, Joseph Moody, was quite taken by her charms, writing in his diary, "I can scarcely keep myself from loving her." His father, Reverend Samuel Moody, disapproved of the match, however. Only a few months later Captain Pepperrell came to call on Miss Hirst; she married Pepperrell shortly thereafter.

Sir William Pepperrell, a Kittery merchant who was briefly governor of Massachusetts, was the first native American to become a baronet — in recognition of his role in the capture of Louisburg, Nova Scotia, during the French and Indian Wars. The carved dolphins over the doorway are reminders that the sea was originally the source of the family's wealth.

Across the street is a tiny Congregational church, one of the prettiest in New England. The parsonage out back is the oldest in Maine. The

church's burying ground, next to the harbor just across the road, has many interesting stones. The old tombstones give a glimpse into Kittery's past, like one marking a communal grave for the crew of the "Hattie Eaton," a brig wrecked off Gerrish Island. Another stone bears an epitaph written by British poet, Robert Browning, for a man he'd never met: Levi Lincoln Thaxter, husband of local poet Celia Thaxter and an admirer of Browning's work. But words, even those chiseled in granite or rough boulder, pale beside the beauty of Spruce Creek — the most fitting memorial for Kittery folk.

A little further eastward, on your right, is an attractive mansard-roofed house, once the summer residence of author and ATLANTIC MONTHLY editor William Dean Howells. Mark Twain was a frequent visitor here, and from "Barnbury" — a combination of unused stable and library — Howells corresponded with notables of his day, like artist Howard Pyle, philosopher William James, and President Theodore Roosevelt.

Ahead on your right is ***Fort McClary State Historic Site***. This compact complex of fortifications, built in the mid-19th century, was originally named Fort Pepperrell, for one of Kittery's most influential citizens — you guessed it, Sir William. To his financial loss, he remained a loyalist to the Crown long after his compatriots supported the Revolution, and the site was renamed Fort McClary, to honor a hero of the Battle of Bunker Hill instead. From the blockhouse the sweeping views of the outer harbor are unsurpassed. *Open June - October; grounds free, small fee for blockhouse. Limited parking.*

If you brought your lunch with you, there's an inviting, well-equipped picnic area sited in a cool pine grove just across the road. Tables overlook a placid pond filled with lilies.

Ahead lies the heart of this tiny village, consisting of a postage-stamp-sized post office, Frisbee's General Store, and CAPTAIN SIMEON'S GALLEY RESTAURANT — an informal place with views of Pepperrell Cove, 207/439-3655. In colonial days, the village was a bustling metropolis, because the town dock was the scene of the Pepperrell family trading activities. The wharves and warehouses are long gone, but the views remain.

Most of the original Pepperrell home stands across from the post office. (It looked more like a mansion before a thirty-foot section was lopped off.) Two houses past the Pepperrell Mansion is the John Bray House — a comfortable dwelling that is the oldest building (1662) still standing in town. John Bray kept a public house here in the 17th century before turning to shipbuilding. His daughter, Margery, married Englishman William Pepperrell, Sr., then the owner of fishing fleets off Newfoundland and the Isles of Shoals, and Bray gave the newlyweds land next to his home on which to build.

Rte. 103 continues to wind up and down and around Kittery Point. After passing a gas station, the road turns sharply to the right. A little further up and down the road you come to Chauncey Creek Rd., also on the right, which you should take if you're still interested in lobster or want to visit Fort Foster and Seapoint Beach. The road skirts the narrow creek, affording appealing views of the dark green water and the pine-studded rocky shore on the other side. If you prefer to eat "al fresco," CHAUNCEY CREEK LOBSTER PIER, 207/439-1030, is a perfect place to indulge — simple and casual, with a deck overlooking the quiet waterway, studded with lobster boats. (You will need to bring your own bottle, however, if you want anything spirited to drink.)

The signs at a lobster pound speak a language all their own: "chix" means chicken lobster (one pound and under), "quarters" refer to shellfish under one-and-a-half pounds; "large" means one-and-a-half to two-and-a-half pounds; "jumbo" over two-and-a-half pounds. Do not soak in water before cooking because they will drown; the water they live in at a pound or seafood store is aerated.

To cook lobster, put two inches of water in a large pot (seawater can be used or simply add salt to tap water). Once the water has reached a rolling boil, gently drop the lobsters head-first into the pot, cover and steam 12-20 minutes, depending on the size.

The white meat from the tail, body and claws is what most people enjoy; however, there are lobstermen who will eat only the tomalley, the green liver, and coral, the red roe. Serve with corn on the cob, lots of napkins, "crackers" and "picks" (those sold for nuts work fine for shellfish). Melted butter is optional — it adds calories and richness that fresh lobster does not require.

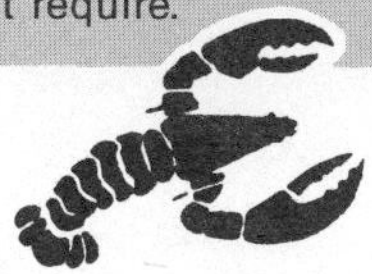

Down the road a piece you will come to an intersection, and if you go right across the bridge you will be on Gerrish Island; go right again and you will be heading toward the beach at the end of the road.

Except for a few houses scattered about, the only activity nowadays takes place at ***Fort Foster***, a large, well-developed park operated by the Town of Kittery. It wasn't always this way; at the turn of the century, travel by railroad and steamship was at its peak, bringing a booming tourism business to summer hotels on Kittery Point and Gerrish Island.

Like all public lands along the coast of New England, Fort Foster is popular on summer weekends. For bathers or wind-surfers, there is a wide strip of hard-packed sand along the river at low tide and a small, rocky beach on the ocean. Naturalists will enjoy several trails through a wide variety of habitats: woodland, river, salt marshes, and ocean. Not to be overlooked are the tidal pools among the rocks — especially for kids who like squirmy things. But mostly people come to Fort Foster to take in the views toward Whaleback Light and New Castle, watching the constantly changing boat traffic along the river. *There are plenty of picnic tables, barbecues, and playing fields. Parking is not always sufficient on hot summer weekends. Small fee.*

To reach ***Seapoint Beach,*** *go back over the Gerrish Island bridge and turn right immediately after the bridge, heading toward the ocean.* This scenic road skirts Chauncey Creek, passing through salt marshes and pine woods, until it comes to an end at Seapoint. In summer, parking is limited to Kittery residents. A solution is to have a friend drop you off while s/he visits the outlet malls. *Return to the gas station on rte. 103 and turn right onto Haley Rd. Rte. 1 is approximately three miles down the road; the outlets are to your left.*

Because of the parking restrictions and limited development along the salt marshes, Seapoint offers quiet isolation most of the time. There are actually two beaches here, separated by a small rocky peninsula. Crescent Beach, to the south, is pebbly, while Seapoint Beach, to the north, is sandy. Together, they are only a half-mile long.

To get back to rte. 103, head back to the Gerrish Island bridge intersection and turn right. At the stop sign turn right onto rte. 103 north toward the Yorks. The road winds through a sparsely populated section of Kittery Point for several miles before arriving at a large body of water, which is York Harbor. In the distance you can see the ocean — the first time the Atlantic can be viewed from the road in Maine.

On the left is a fir-studded point, connected to the mainland by a tiny suspension bridge and a rock causeway. The rough trail around this point will give weary travelers a chance to stretch their legs, while exploring a small coniferous ecosystem. *There is no parking lot here, but you can usually find enough space along the road to leave your car.*

You may want to keep the tides and moon in mind, though. Our family discovered this inviting trail one fine spring day and had no trouble crossing the causeway to the point, but were forced to wade through icy water coming back — thanks to an especially high tide, caused by a full moon.

The Yorks.

This cluster of coastal communities has everything you might want — and more! Historic charm, sand beaches, attractive inns, huge mansions, even a trailer park with ocean views can be found here. For summer visitors, trolley service connects the beach with the village. *Call the York Chamber of Commerce for details, 207/363-4422.*

York was part of the early Province of Maine, Sir Fernando Gorges' would-be feudal kingdom in the new world, until the Massachusetts Bay Colony took it over in 1652. Like Kittery and Wells, the town saw plenty of fighting. Because the French and Indian War lasted for almost a century, some settlers spent their entire lives under the constant threat of siege, literally growing up in garrisons, those unique New England structures where the second story protrudes out from the first — allowing defending settlers to put out fires and preventing easy access. By 1691 York, Kittery, and Wells were the only towns remaining in what would become the state of Maine — frequent Indian raids had prevented colonists from growing enough crops to sustain themselves elsewhere.

There's a wealth of history inland for those who are ready to savor it (see sidetrips that follow and on page 78). Or if you prefer to continue toward the ocean, you can stop enroute at the ***Sayward-Wheeler House***, 79 Barrell Lane, 207/363-2709, visible to your right just above the harbor. Remodeled

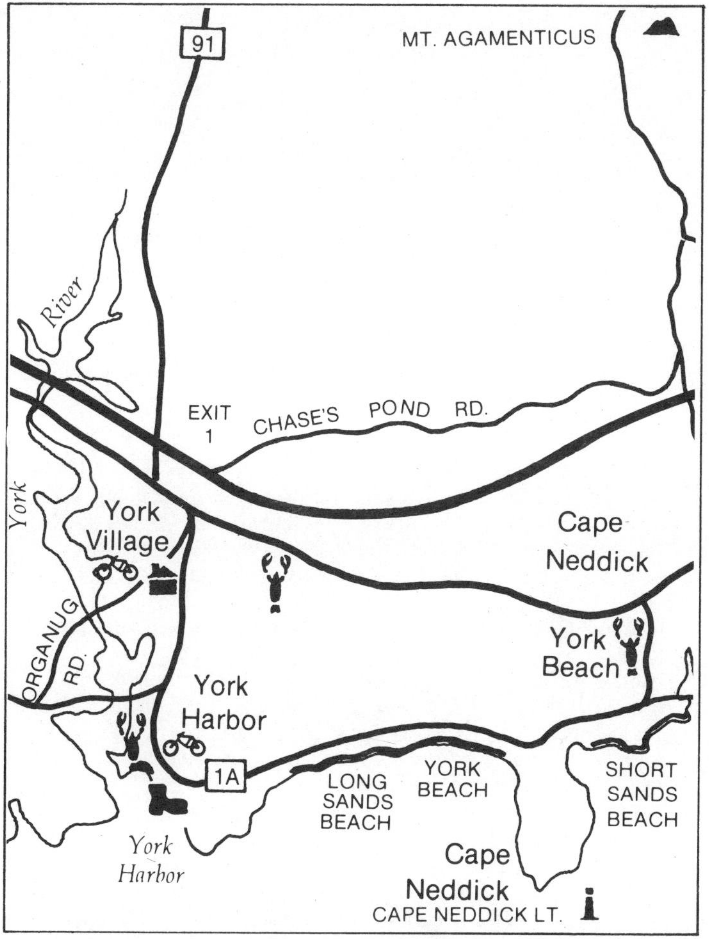

in the 1760s by merchant and Judge Jonathan Sayward, this home contains Queen Anne and Chippendale antiques as well as booty brought back from the expedition against the French at Louisburg, Nova Scotia in 1745. *Continue on rte. 103 past the water to the first right, Barrell Ln. Go up the hill and again take the first right onto Barrell Ln. Ext. The house is on the right, halfway down the hill. Open mid-June — mid-October; admission.*

> In the 17th century York was physically a garrison town — no one capable of soldiering could leave without paying a fine or "gaol."

Sidetrip: ***York Village***. Just beyond the harbor you will come to a stop sign, where rte. 103 ends at rte. 1A. Turn left, if you'd like to spend some time stepping back into York's colorful past. The Old York Historical Society, located in the George Marshall Store, 140 Lindsay Road, 207/363-4975, maintains a wide spectrum of properties that give a good idea of the scope of colonial architecture along this coast. *Open June 20-October 1 with costumed guides; frequent historical skits and various demonstrations of early American crafts are given as well. Tickets to all the restored buildings can be purchased here; discounts for seniors and children. Weekend group tours may be arranged in spring and fall.*

Follow rte. 1A through the center of town, past the Civil War Memorial soldier. Take a left on Lindsay Road with its cluster of quaint buildings. ***Jefferd's Tavern***, just off rte. 1A, houses an orientation center and will also sell you tickets for any of York's restorations. Originally

> During colonial times every village was required by law to maintain an inn for travellers. The General Court of Massachusetts prescribed strict rules regarding food, drink, and prices in this part of the seacoast; no dancing or card playing was allowed in the 17th century.

a stop on the King's Highway in Wells, this 18th century inn was moved here in 1939, using original materials whenever possible. *Gift shop; weaving and cooking demonstrations.*

The Old Burying Ground is outside. Look for the grave of Mary Nason, for years believed a witch because a heavy stone slab, presumably to keep her buried, covered her grave. Some suggest the large rock was put here instead by the widower, to prevent wandering livestock from grazing on his wife's resting place; certainly the head- and footstones are unlikely memorials to a witch. Judge Jonathan Sayward, who was York's richest man when he died in 1797, and Jeremiah Moulton, a noted Indian fighter, are buried here too.

The ***Emerson-Wilcox House***, right on 1A, was built in 1742 and has served as general store, tavern, tailor's shop, post office, and home. 18th-century crewelwork bedhangings, made by York's Mary Bulman, and the tap room are of interest here. Although it may be under restoration when you visit, the ***Old Gaol***, just across Lindsay Road on 1A, is always fun for children — look for 'pass-throughs', where firewood and food could be

Massachusetts-born Peter Weare was put in York's Gaol in the 17th century for political trouble-making. Complaining "I found nothing but ye flore to ly upon," he convinced his jailer to take him home where he could be guarded more comfortably.

shoved into cells without opening a door, and the 'trip-stair', built a few inches higher than others to slow escaping prisoners. There is also a collection of early American toys and clothing.

The Old Schoolhouse, just off 1A, was built in 1745 and is the oldest surviving such building in the nation. The exhibit "Good Common Schools" explains the kind of education students in the Cider Hill School District received in the 18th and 19th centuries.

The next group of buildings is a short distance away, though far enough to warrant driving or biking. Continue west along 1A to Organug Road, just before the York Street Baptist Church and notice the triangular-shaped grassy spot at the intersection. This is called *a heaterpiece.* Back in colonial days, wagons carting mast pines couldn't negotiate sharp-angled turns, like this one, so intersections were built with Y-shapes rather than T-shapes. Throughout the back roads of New England, you'll often notice heaterpieces.

Follow Organug Road through a residential neighborhood and the fairways of the York Golf and Tennis Club, to Lindsay Road on the left. Continue straight here, crossing over Sewall's Bridge to the ***Elizabeth Perkins House***, one of the few homes to have escaped the massacre of 1692. The original house has been moved and is hardly recognizable in the Victorian home that remains, although parts of the colonial dwelling are believed to have been used in the present dining room. Interpreted as a 20th-century dwelling, the Perkins House may be of particular interest to anyone involved in restoring an old home. *Old-fashioned teas are served in the afternoon.*

Returning over the bridge, turn right onto Lindsay Road for your last stop. The famous patriot was part-owner of the ***John Hancock Warehouse***, located right on the York River. One of Maine's oldest commercial buildings, it now houses an exhibit explaining how important the York River and its wharves were for 250 years. The Historical Society's headquarters are next door in the ***George Marshall Store*** that also served as a chandlery and customs house in the days when York's wharves were busier than its roads. Nearby is Wiggley Bridge, where pedestrians can watch the tide flow under their swaying feet. (Ask at the Historical Society for directions.)

The first undershot mill, where wheels are turned by tidal pressure on the bottom, rather than the flow over the top of the wheel, was on the York River.

Follow Lindsay Rd. back to rte. 1A to return to the scenic drive along the coast. Or if you'd like to see even more old homes (privately-owned), take Indian Trail Road, a left-turn off Lindsay Road, back to Organug and then turn right on 1A, heading toward York Harbor.

Just before the rte. 103 intersection, you may notice a sign on the left for BILL FOSTER'S DOWNEAST CLAMBAKE, 207/363-3255. His informal restaurant serves fresh clams, lobsters, Maine potatoes, and corn cooked over seaweed, as well as less traditional clam-bake fare five evenings a week in the season. There are swings and horseshoes out back. It's fun to come early and watch *the clambake being prepared. Reservations required, although they can often be made early on the day you want to eat here.*

A Summer Home for the Rich and Famous

If you choose the scenic route, just turn right where rte. 103 runs into rte. 1A. There are plenty of interesting sights here as well. ***York Harbor***, just ahead, is a prosperous community of attractive homes, some carefully sited to capture water views.

York Harbor has long attracted the elite: John Jacob Astor, Harvard President Charles Eliot, Mark Twain, John Greenleaf Whittier, Maine Senator and Presidential candidate James Blaine all summered here.

For a closer look at some of them and a walk along the rocky shore, head right, at the sign for THE STAGE NECK INN, 207/363-3850, an attractive, modern complex of resort hotel and condominiums overlooking both the harbor and the ocean. *You want to drive straight down Harbor Beach Rd., rather than heading right toward the Inn. Two-hour parking is available on 1A or along Harbor Beach Rd.* Walk down, almost to the water, looking for the ***Cliff Walk*** to your left. The sidewalk may need repair in places along the two-mile path, especially after a hard winter, but it will lead to spectacular views. Or you can go in the other direction, across the Stage Neck Inn road and take the ***Wharf Walk***, which goes up the York River next to the still active docks and warehouses.

Back up Harbor Beach Rd. on rte. 1A, you'll see the YORK HARBOR INN, 207/363-5119, on your left, a delightfully old-fashioned place to sleep or dine. The extensive dinner menu ranges from beef tenderloin topped with crabmeat, asparagus, and bernaise sauce to shrimp and scallops served with angel hair pasta.

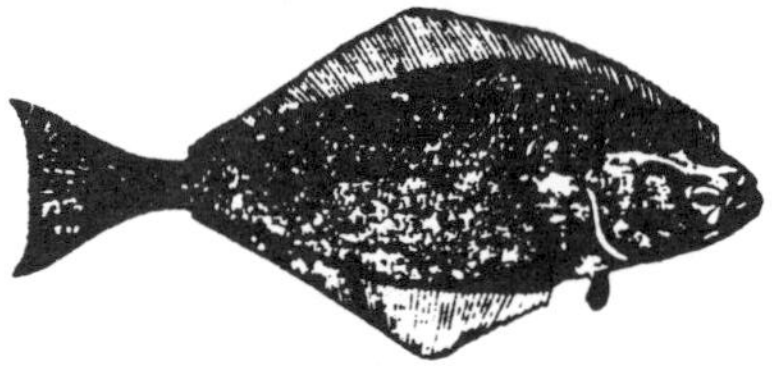

Sidetrip: Seabury Charters, Inc., 207/363-5675; substantial fee. For a day of real fishing — spent either alongside commercial fishermen or in a group of your choosing — the waters off York Harbor offer real adventure. If you're lucky enough to catch a bluefin tuna, the captain will split the sale with you (and you can afford to buy your own boat or pay for more charters).

Many popular gamefish winter from Cape Hatteras to the Florida Keys, moving into these northern waters as the southern Atlantic becomes too warm: Atlantic mackerel, followed by blues, flukes, weakfish; then in summer come tuna, bonito, dolphin, marlin, tarpon, mako sharks, groupers, and barracuda.

Continuing along 1A, you may want to stay close to the ocean. *If so, turn right at Norwood Farms Road (there's a good-sized sign for Harbor Home just above the street sign). This residential street leads you as close as you can get to the Atlantic, although you will have to share the view with the owners of ocean-front properties. Turn left at the bottom of Norwood Farms Road and you'll make a loop onto Roaring Rock Road and back to 1A.* Once you pass a trailer park, you'll know you're in ***York Beach***, a major summer colony, composed of midriff-to-elbow cottages and carryouts.

Look for the figure-head of a woman on your left; she's the sign for THE WINDBREAKER, 207/363-3807, past the Anchorage Motel. While breakfast is fine, dinner is downright gourmet, with Mimmo in the kitchen and Diane out front to help you decide just how you want your Fettucine Sinatra — mild, spicy, or really hot? Bring your own bottle (they supply ice and wine glasses as well as corkage) and settle down to some of the best Italian cooking north of Boston. If this restaurant is full, there's another excellent Italian eatery nearby.

Sidetrip: FAZIO'S, 207/363-7019, York Village. Go back rte. 1A to Long Sands Rd., which will take you to this small restaurant in the York Village Shopping Plaza on your left. Mama Fazio's speciality sauce and homemade pasta are available for lunch, dinner, or take-out. Whether you choose the roasted peppers, veal and herb ravioli, or seafood lasagne, the cooking is both innovative and wholesome.

Beaches, Beaches, Beaches.

Now there's nothing between you and the ocean but ***Long Sands Beach*** — one mile long but often so crowded that it's hard to find the sand. *Metered parking is limited to the right side of 1A, which means it's usually non-existent on beach days.* The lighthouse you can see from here is ***Nubble Light.***

Sidetrip: ***Cape Neddick***. Take the first right after Long Sands Beach, Nubble Rd., out to the lighthouse. When the Coast Guard built Nubble Light in 1879, a real decline in shipwrecks resulted. Today it remains a classic-looking lighthouse with its spare New England buildings and surf breaking up behind the Nubble. Although the park itself is not much more than the parking lot and a few telescopes, some 100,000 visitors stop here each year. *To get back to 1A, take a right from Sohier Park Rd., making a loop along Broadway to 1A.*

Continuing northward, you will come to ***Short Sands Beach***, a quarter-mile crescent that serves another summer crowd. The center of York Beach is up ahead — about as much a contrast to York Harbor as you could ask for. For arcades, souvenir shopping, and people-watching, this is the place. *Playground, limited parking.*

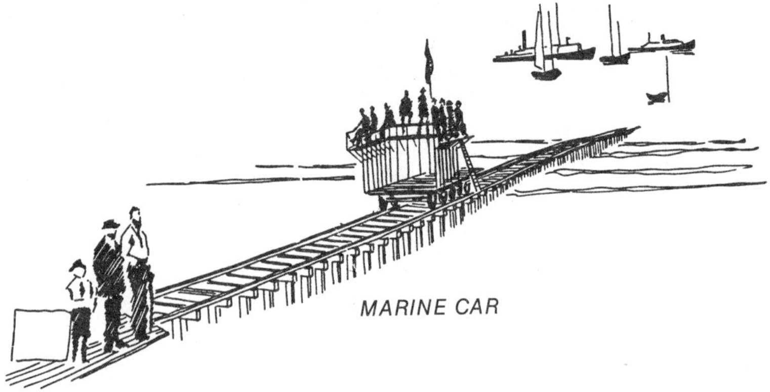

MARINE CAR

The Portsmouth, Dover, and York St. Railway, known more affectionately as "Pull, Drag, and Yank" had to defeat an injunction brought against it by affluent York Harbor residents, but it eventually ran through the Yorks.

Factory and mill workers came to York Beach whenever they could afford it. In 1889 a "marine car" on rails carried passengers out to sea for a thrilling ride.

After creeping through this busy part of York Beach, rte. 1A turns inland (see restaurants listed on inland sidetrips, page 78), eventually hooking up with rte. 1, while Shore Rd. veers off to the

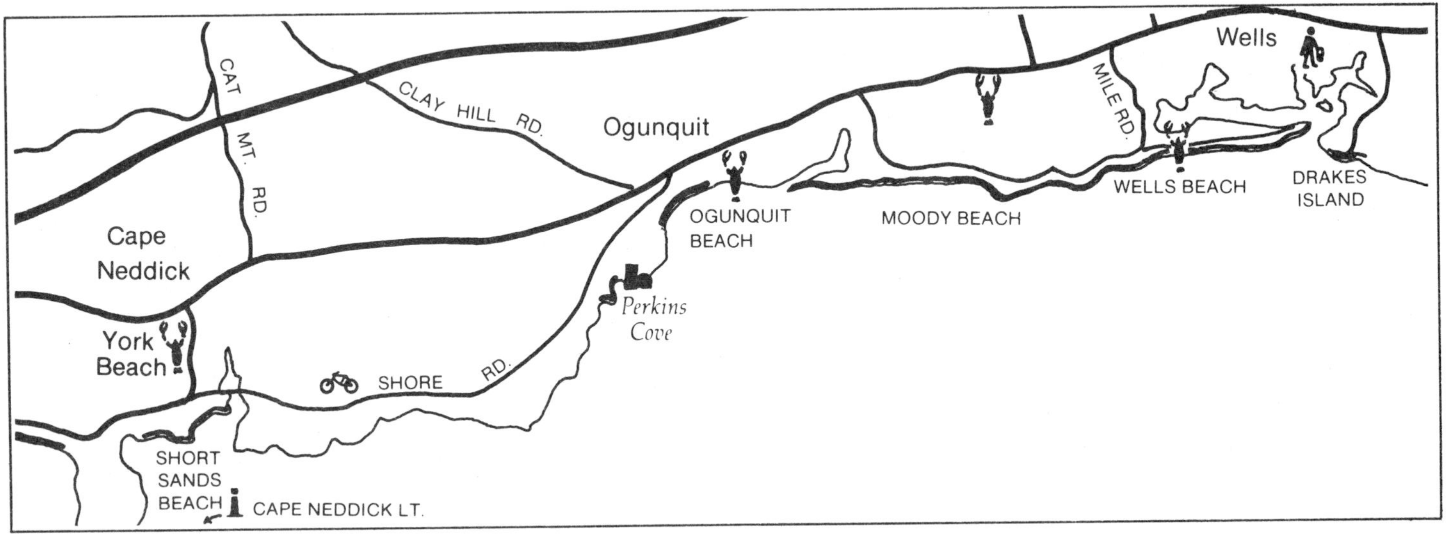

right, hugging the coastline. We recommend taking this road, for it passes through some incredible scenery enroute to Ogunquit. *Agamenticus Ave., a right off Shore Rd., offers especially memorable sights.*

The further north you go, the more interesting this road becomes — with woods, rock outcroppings, and pounding surf that may spray you if your window is down or if you're biking. Just before entering a thickly settled area, you will pass through a pine-studded landscape littered with huge boulders, evidence of the ice sheet that covered northern New England thousands of years ago.

About 12,000 years ago the last of five major ice sheets, covering the northern half of New England, melted. As this occurred, the land which had been depressed by the weight of the ice was flooded, and clay deposited in the process. In this area today, deposits of light brown clay run 20 miles wide and may have risen as much as 500 feet above sea level.

Since the ice sheets were believed to have been two miles thick, glacial meltdown was significant. The huge boulders you see scattered about the landscape here and in other areas along the coast are from this period; broken-off pieces of rock were transported south by what was left of the melting ice sheet, though they rarely traveled more than a few miles. Early settlers had hard work clearing fields, but boulders and rocks provided ample material for building chimneys and fences.

The weathered building on the right that looks hand-carved is the Museum of Art, 207/646-4909, with exhibits of local artists' work, past and present. *Free; open only in season.*

Beautiful Place by the Sea.

Even before you come to the beach, you'll realize why the Indians named ***Ogunquit*** "beautiful place by the sea." Today attractive galleries, shops, restaurants, and homes complement the natural beauty. For a walk along the coast, browsing, or a boat trip, turn right at the stop sign to ***Perkins Cove.*** *Limited parking; however, several restaurants here have their own lots, if you're hungry as well. Molly's Trolleys provide inexpensive, reliable transportation: "Molly, Wally, Polly, and Dolly" make a four mile loop up and down rte. 1, through Ogunquit village, Perkins Cove, and down to the beach all summer long; minimal fee. 207/646-5908.*

THE WHISTLING OYSTER, 207/646-9521, is the most up-scale eatery on the Cove, built to capture the views. The kitchen uses fresh herbs freely and concentrates as much on how a dish looks as on taste. If you're feeling flush, there are fresh oysters with dill sauce, scallops seviche, and marinated swordfish served with coriander butter.

BARNACLE BILLY'S LOBSTER POUND, 207/646-5575, next door offers serve-yourself seafood on its patio or in the noisy dining room. Closer to the other end of the price-scale, this eatery is so popular that you may need to wait in line — to get in, to order, to use the bathrooms.

Past the public parking lot is a cluster of attractive boutiques and galleries, often even a painter or two at work. In the cove itself is a fleet of lobster boats, at least one of which takes visitors along to watch the lobstermen at work.

Sidetrip: ***Finestkind Scenic Cruises***, 207/646-5227, runs 50-minute lobstering trips that are ideal for families. A narrator explains lobstering techniques, and kids get to handle banded arthropods or bring home a starfish. *Admission; operates June-October. Also cocktail cruises and longer trips to Nubble Light; refreshments.*

On the ocean side of the parking lot, there's a half-mile path that winds between huge beach "cottages" and the surf. ***The Marginal Way*** is probably the best-maintained of the coast's many pathways — paved, with handrails and numerous benches. The path winds from Perkins Cove to the south end of Ogunquit Beach with plenty of places where youngsters can climb on the rocks or explore tidal pools. A moonlight stroll here is unforgettable. *Sneakers advised for exploring the rocks.*

The road from the Cove to the village leads past an interesting Italian restaurant, ROBERTO'S, 207/646-8130. Although you may feel squeezed even if you're able to get a reservation, the scampi and the veal make it all worthwhile.

Ogunquit has long been an artists' colony, attracting the likes of Walt Kuhn (whose paintings were recently the subject of a one-man show at New York's Whitney Museum) and Marsden Hartley. The Barn Gallery is perhaps the best-known of the many you'll find here. Broadway theatre is another feature of this attractive community. In the 1930s the Manhattan Repertoire Colony brought first-rate theatre here; the Ogunquit Playhouse, rte. 1, 207/646-5511, opens the end of June for the summer season.

The intersection of Perkins Cove Rd. with rte. 1 is in a class by itself. Depending on where you're coming from and where you're going, you have to be aggressive, defensive, and lucky at the same time. Our suggestion is to take a sharp right toward nearby ***Ogunquit Beach***. Close to a mile of ashtray-fine sand make this a sunbathing connoisseur's dream. *Small admission; ample parking lot.* Return to rte. 1 in the village for some of the best New York style sandwiches, and perhaps the only lox and bagels in this part of Maine at EINSTEIN'S DELI, 2 Shore Rd., 207/646-5262, on the south side of the intersection.

There are interesting inland trips from this area (see Sidetrips Section, page 77), though if the weather's good you may prefer to continue along the coast. You'll pass numerous restaurants and motels along rte. 1, and the further north you go, the more congested traffic gets. At certain times of day, cars move slower than the dog who carried mail to Wells years ago.

To avoid some of this congestion, turn right by the flashing light at the large sign for Moody Beach. In just a minute you'll find yourself at the southern end of a seven-mile stretch of sand serving densely-populated summer colonies. ***Moody and Wells Beaches*** are wide enough to handle the crowds at low tide, but when the sea rolls in, sunbathers may have to retreat to the seawall, rocks, or their rented beach houses. *Facilities and fee parking at both beaches. Trolley service that connects with Ogunquit trolleys, 207/646-2451.*

Wells, the Easternmost Garrison.

Along the road between the two beaches you will come to one of our favorite restaurants, THE GRAY GULL INN, 321 Webhannet Dr., 207/646-7501. Located in a comfortable old beach house, the inn offers views of rocks in the ocean where seals can be seen. Veal chops with sausage, huge but tender scampi, and interesting salads make for gourmet dining, while breakfast is a pleasant meal here too.

After passing through the southern half of Wells Beach, you will come to a stop sign. Turn left here onto Mile Road, which will take you back to rte. 1 and the center of Wells.

Mile Road passes through an extensive salt marsh, which separates the rte. 1 commercial strip from the beach. The salt marsh is not only home to many shorebirds, but is also the site of many splendid sunsets. A good place to watch the sun set is from the deck at BILLY'S CHOWDER HOUSE, on the right, 207/646-7558. For casual meals (lobster roll or haddock sandwich) at a good price, Billy's is hard to beat, as the number of cars in the parking lot attests. *When you reach the stop light at rte. 1, turn right.*

After turning, look for the ***Wells Antique Auto Museum*** on the right. Dad may be more interested than the kids in the 1904 Stanley Steamer, which has a raised seat for the driver, or the 1963 Studebaker Skylark, but your children are sure to find something here that intrigues them from the collection of nickelodeons and old-fashioned pin-ball machines. There are even hand-cranked moving pictures, like "Rin Tin Tin," "The Lure of Youth," or "The Exotic Mirror Dance" — pretty tame stuff compared to today's MTV! *Open late May—mid-September, admission. 207/646-9064.*

Sidetrip: ***Teasel Weed Herb Farm***, Bragdon's Crossing, 207/646-5172. Old-fashioned perennials — the kind you remember from Grandmother's garden — and a wealth of herbs make a nice excursion for flower-lovers. Darr Littlefield-Fortin has spent twenty years learning about native east-coast plants and has four attractive raised beds for visitors' inspection: an early American perennial garden filled with bedstraw (which our ancestors used to fill their pillows), heliotrope, non-stinging nettle, miniature delphinium, or patchouli; a tea garden with Clary sage, hyssops, hibiscus, and scented geraniums; a traditional kitchen garden full of lovage (the stalks of which are sold to local restaurants as "straws" for sipping Bloody Marys) as well as parsley, sage, rosemary, and thyme. There is also a "white witch's garden" full of the kinds of medicinal herbs with which New England's early healers treated everything from fever to nervous disorders. *Turn diagonally left onto Bragdon Road just beyond the Auto Museum. After about a mile, take a diagonal left onto a dirt road. The gardens are on your right next to the last house on this road. To return to rte. 1, continue north on Bragdon Rd. to the stop sign at rte. 9. Turn right and you will reach rte. 1 in about one mile. For those in a hurry, just take a left instead; I-95 and the Maine Turnpike are about a half mile ahead.*

This section of rte. 1 is one area you may want to drive through slowly — antique shops, cut-rate factory outlets, and used-book stores abound. If you're hungry, there are also several food stops worth taking. For handcrafted sandwiches, try THE HITCH, 207/646-9229, on the right just beyond the high school. There is a small dining area for light lunches, but really this restaurant is an ideal spot to pick up picnic fare for the beach. If you're looking for a complete meal, turn right from rte. 1 onto Landing Rd., just beyond the stoplight at rte. 9, and head east to Wells Harbor. Here you'll find LORD'S SEAFOOD RESTAURANT, 207/646-2651, overlooking the salt marsh. Whether you're interested in boiled lobster or a delicious lobster roll, this is a good place to find them.

Bargain hunters may want to keep their eyes peeled for the Wells Union Antique Center on the right. Further along is Cole's Corner Country Mall on the left after the flashing light at Laudholm Rd. Just past Drakes Island Rd., you'll come to LITCHFIELD'S SEAFOOD RESTAURANT, 207/646-5711. This is where the locals eat, and for good reason — the raw bar and fish 'n chips are among the best around and reasonably priced.

As you proceed north, the area seems less commercial, and it's easier to imagine what Wells might have been like in the past. The settlement officially became a town in 1653 and welcomed British colonists whose homes and forts were destroyed elsewhere by frequent Indian raids, although some of the bloodiest attacks took place here. The French paid their Indian allies for hostages from these coastal towns; Esther Wheelwright, a Protestant child whom the savages took captive in Wells in 1703 and marched to Canada, eventually became Mother Superior of the Ursuline Convent in Quebec.

Wells' original settlers lived in log houses, slept on mattresses made of cattail rushes, and dined without benefit of crockery or glassware. Nevertheless, they were good fighters. By 1690 Indian attacks left Wells the last frontier to the English settlement of New England. In one battle at Lt. Joseph Storer's garrison here, 29 soldiers from Massachusetts plus a few Wells settlers succeeded in holding off 400 French and Indian attackers.

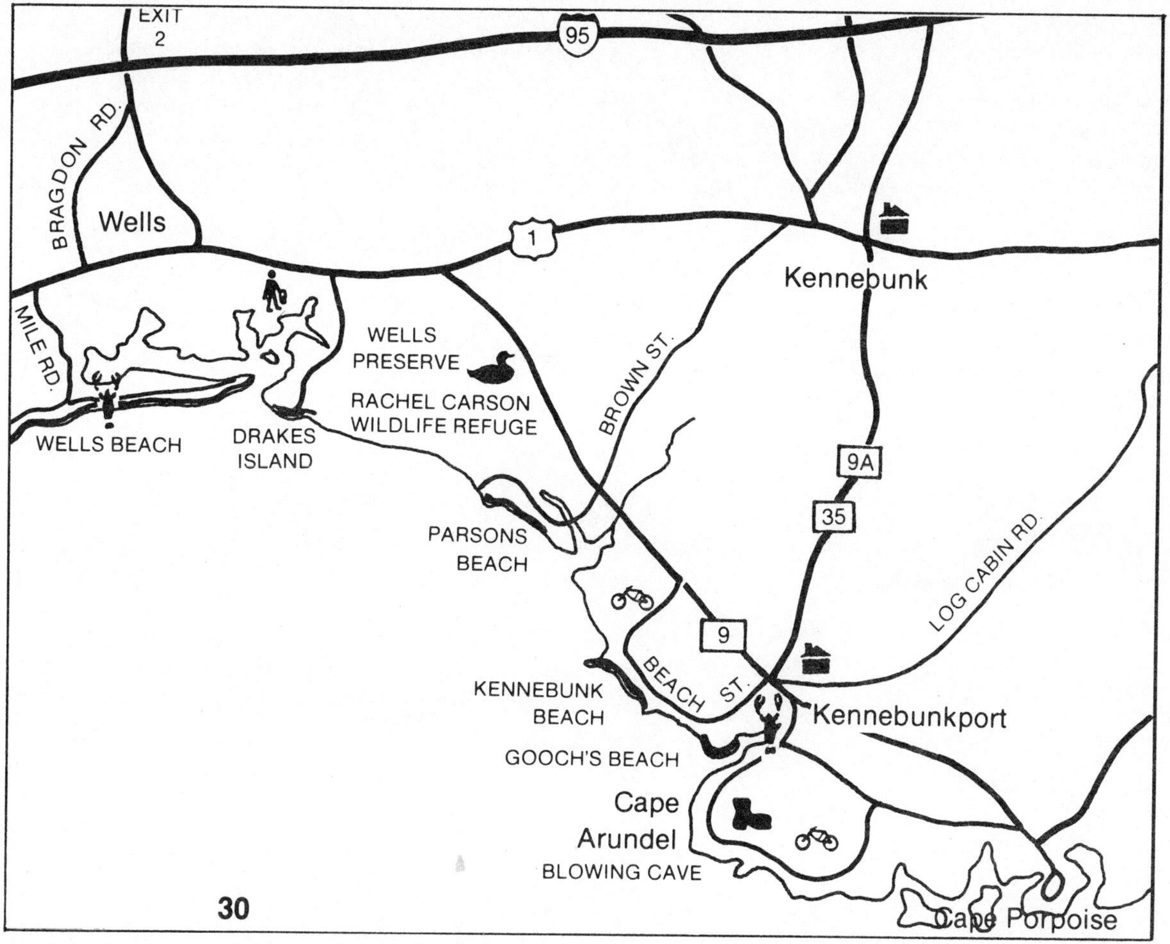
EXIT
2
95
BRAGDON RD.
Wells
1
MILE RD.
Kennebunk
WELLS
PRESERVE
RACHEL CARSON
WILDLIFE REFUGE
BROWN ST.
WELLS BEACH
DRAKES
ISLAND
9A
35
PARSONS
BEACH
LOG CABIN RD.
9
BEACH ST.
KENNEBUNK
BEACH
Kennebunkport
GOOCH'S BEACH
Cape
Arundel
BLOWING CAVE
30
Cape Porpoise

GREATER
YELLOWLEGS

Sidetrip: ***The Wells Reserve and Laudholm Farm.*** This 1500-acre tract of meadows, orchards, fields, and salt marshes includes two estuaries and covers nine miles of seashore. Three different properties — the Rachel Carson Wildlife Refuge, Laudholm Farm, and undeveloped park land belonging to the state of Maine — make up what has been called "the most ambitious environmental project on the North Atlantic Coast." Through private fundraising and matching federal dollars, Laudholm Farm, in the middle, was purchased in 1986 to complete the Wells Reserve.

In 1881 George C. Lord, the former president of the Boston & Maine Railroad bought the 270-acre estate and developed it into an experimental farming showcase, where state-of-the-art Victorian technology was demonstrated. Even a private railroad station was built for the convenience of visitors. Today efforts are underway to adapt the farm as a visitor center for the public. For scientists, scholars and professional naturalists, the Reserve will serve as a research and education center in estuarine biology. An extensive trail network provides visitors with access to a variety of wildlife habitats. *Turn right on Laudholm Farm Rd. at the flashing light and look for signs and the headquarters building on the left. Access and visitor center hours vary. To avoid disappointment, call ahead of time. 207/646-4521.*

Back on rte. 1, look for rte. 9 bearing off to your right, just past the MAINE DINER, 207/646-4441, a good place for a cup of coffee and a blueberry muffin. About a mile down this wooded residential road, you can momentarily exchange civilization for quiet woods, still ponds, and salt marshes teeming with life. On your right is the ***Rachel Carson Wildlife Refuge.***

You can show your appreciation of the seacoast's natural beauty by making a contribution to one of the many wildlife preserves or Audubon Society sanctuaries. Volunteer and nonprofit groups help make this area an attractive place for us all; they benefit from donations — small or large.

Park along the road near the headquarters building to hike the one-mile circular trail here. This main trail is an easy walk even for young children or seniors, clearly marked, and shadily cool on the warmest days. Part of the trail turns to boardwalk over the marsh, an important feeding ground for larval clams and lobsters, Maine crabs and fish. Birders can expect to find a wide variety of songbirds, marshbirds, and ducks. Longer trails branch off from the main loop. *Open year-round, free. 207/646-9064.*

One of my favorite approaches to a . . . seacoast is by a rough path through an evergreen forest that has its own peculiar enchantment." Rachel Carson 1955.

Proceeding north on rte. 9, after passing the Idealease Motel on your left, look for Parsons Beach Rd. on your right, for one of the nicest swimming spots around. This country road may feel more like Virginia horse country than rural Maine, but there is a beautiful mile-long stretch of white sand at the end. There are actually two beaches: ***Crescent Beach*** to the south and ***Parsons Beach*** to the north. *They are rarely crowded and for good reason: parking is practically nonexistent. Unless you are very lucky, you'll need a friend, who would rather explore Kennebunk or the Port, to drop you off. No picnic tables, no changing houses, just marsh and beach — still pretty much the way God made them.*

"Crabs of thumbnail size live in the weed and come down to hunt in these areas. They are the young of the green crab; the adults live below the tide lines on this shore except when they come into the shelter of the weeds to molt. The young crabs search the mud pockets, digging out pits and probing for clams that are about their own size.

"Clams, crabs, and worms are part of a community of animals whose lives are closely interrelated. The crabs and the worms are the active predators, the beasts of prey. The clams, the mussels, and the barnacles are the plankton feeders, able to live sedentary lives because their food is brought to them by each tide. By an immutable law of nature, the plankton feeders as a group are more numerous than those that prey on them." Rachel Carson from THE ROCKY COAST.

FULL-RIGGED SHIP

The Kennebunks.

To get back to civilization follow Brown St., the left turn after the Idealease Motel, through pine woods for close to three miles. A nice biking road, it runs past a National Wildlife Refuge, an old burying ground, and a trailer decorated with hubcaps — taking you into ***Kennebunk***. This attractive town developed from shipbuilding and trade with the West Indies. In the era of clipper ships, there were 50 shipyards in the area. Today huge, gracious homes reflect Kennebunk's rich past, while bustling shops, inns, and restaurants suggest the area's popularity.

The Lafayette Center, across rte. 1 from Brown St., combines historical ambience and modern commercialism in a pleasing way. Further along rte. 1 on your right is the KENNEBUNK INN, 207/985-3351, a homey, comfortable place to stay and/or eat. A bulletin board displays recent thank-you notes from guests; the chocolate "moose" and peanut-butter pie are unbeatable.

Further ahead on the right is the ***Brick Store Museum*** at 117 Main St., actually three 19th century commercial buildings with informative exhibits of fine and decorative arts from the Kennebunks' seafaring past. During the summer of 1987, for example, the museum focused on John Bourne, one of the earliest and most successful shipbuilders and merchants here. Through the efforts of his wife and 15 children, Bourne was one merchant who survived the Embargo, largely through various cottage industries in his home. Architectural walking tours of downtown Kennebunk leave from here every Friday, although groups may call in advance to arrange private tours. *Open Tuesday-Saturday, 10 am-4:30 pm; admission. 207/985-4802.* On the corner is the Brick Store Exchange, an arts and crafts co-op with a wide range of quality merchandise, all handmade.

During the shipbuilding days, the residents of coastal towns were as cosmopolitan as anyone anywhere. If a Kennebunker hadn't actually sailed to some part of the known globe, s/he had a relative or friend who had. Whaling was carried on only sparingly in this area; cargo ships were far more important. Homes along the coast were filled with the cultural bric-a-brac of that trade: Chinese silk or export porcelain, European music boxes, shawls from India.

Diagonally across the street is the ***First Parish Church*** (1772) with a steeple based on an Asher Benjamin design, and a bell Paul Revere forged in Boston's North End. One of the prettiest of all New England churches, this building was expanded in the early 19th century by cutting it in half and moving the rear section back 28 feet to allow for new construction. *Tours on Thursday afternoons; free. Call 207/985-3700 for further information.*

Turn right from Main Street, heading east on rte. 35/9A, and you'll pass many impressive homes of the Kennebunks' shipbuilding past. ***The Taylor-Barry House***, 24 Summer St., is a classic Federal home with a low-hipped roof, large double chimneys, and fan-shaped windows over the doors.

Built in 1803 by Thomas Eaton, a master builder who was obviously taken with the ideas of Scottish architect Robert Adam, the home boasts original stenciling attributed to Eaton's brother, Moses, an itinerant painter of the period. *Open Tuesday-Thursday, mid-June—mid-October, admission fee. Part of the Brick Store Museum walking tour; for more information, call 207/985-4802.* Further along on the left you'll pass a cream and white confection, known as the Wedding Cake House. Tradition says the intricate ornamentation was added by a ship's captain to give his bride the wedding cake she never had.

Speaking of the Wedding Cake House, travel writer Louise D. Rich quipped, "I hope the bride appreciated this gesture. Personally, I'd scalp any man who did that to any house he expected me to live in."

"The Port."

The road takes you into the Port, as Kennebunkport is known, and as you continue east, the area takes on a marvelous resort feeling with stylish shops and restaurants.

Sidetrip: ***Gooch's and Kennebunk Beach***. Keep straight at the traffic light, if you're ready for the beach, which is less than a mile away. You'll see a Franciscan monastery on the left, then you cross over a bridge to the coast. Gooch's Beach is a fine place to explore tidal pools or collect shorebird feathers. Further along is a small sand beach, named Kennebunk. *Parking is limited at both beaches. Either road inland will take you back to rte. 9. Take another right and you'll end up at the stop light. Head straight across for the Port.*

There's a fine restaurant in the attractive group of shops on the left side of rte. 9 just before the light. Original works by local artists, live piano music, unusual pricing (a bottle of wine for $14.72, dessert for $1.94) make CAFE TOPHER, 207/967-5009, an interesting place — and the food matches the atmosphere. Fresh shrod, lightly breaded; scallops with brie and almonds; chicken baked with honey are good choices here — veal and shrimp are chef's specials daily. This is one restaurant that really seems to know what it's doing!

If you're coming from Kennebunk, turn left at the traffic light and cross over the Kennebunk River, looking for a small eagle statue or a white-washed marker. This is Dock Square, a concentration of boutiques and shops worthy of browsing. If you can't find parking behind the Dock Square Market, continue straight up rte. 9 to the stop sign. *Be careful here — traffic coming from the right doesn't have to stop, as you do. Once you have found a parking place, In-Town Trolleys, a narrated shuttle service, will take you around the port and beaches, or along Ocean Ave. Small fee; 207/967-3686.*

ALISSON'S, 207/967-4841, on the left at Dock Square, is popular with the younger crowd and a lively place for breakfast, lunch, or dinner. For more stylish dining, there's THE KENNEBUNKPORT INN, 207/967-2621, popular with locals and tourists alike. Whether it's butterfly pancakes for breakfast or lobster stuffed with scallops, shrimp, and crab, the Inn does a nice job.

If you go straight past the marker, and turn onto Maine St., you may find parking down one of the many shady side streets. This area is a little quieter than Dock Square and a nice place to stroll. Artists have been naturally attracted to the Kennebunks for generations, and you may find just the watercolor or etching that captures this area best for you right along here.

Painters are not the only artists who have found the coast to their liking: ". . . numerous authors of distinction, literally colonies of them in some instances, notably at York Harbor and Kennebunkport . . . have established vacation homes in Maine and . . . come here summer after summer. If we can count them neither as native writers nor as adopted sons and daughters of Maine, we can at least point in almost every case to the direct influence of Maine on their writings." State librarian Henry E. Dunnack, 1920.

If you'd rather bike or drive than shop, turn right at the stop sign and continue straight for a mile of wonderful old homes, inns, a church that's now condos, and the magnificent Kenneth Roberts estate — the fields and woods to the right. This road will eventually hook up with the coastal route (see below).

Sidetrip: ***Seashore Trolley Museum.*** If you have youngsters in tow, you may want to turn left at the stop sign, instead, heading west of town to the Seashore Trolley Museum, 207/967-2712. Containing the largest collection of old street cars in America, this open-air museum was founded by a group of aficionados who rode the last cars on the Biddeford & Saco Electric Railroad. *Open daily late April to late October; admission. Visitor center, display barn, and renovation shop. Rides on three miles of track. Continue out of town for approximately three miles on North St., which turns into Log Cabin Rd., and the museum will be on the right.*

The Rock-Bound Coast.

By turning right at the white marker in Dock Square you will be on Ocean Ave., heading toward Cape Arundel. ARUNDEL WHARF, 207/967-3444, on the water to your right has pleasant dockside dining, if you're looking for a shrimp roll or a burger. Just past the shops on the left, you'll see a handsome home set back from the street — THE CAPTAIN LORD MANSION, 207/967-3141, a bed-and-breakfast inn furnished in antiques. Further along the water, just before the many yachts, you may notice the Maritime Museum on your right, 207/967-4195, an interesting collection of ship's models, old instruments, and paintings. *Open end of April-November; admission. Antique shop.*

Two large turn-of-the-century hotels are reminders of the past, while attractive restorations and new condominium complexes bring us into the present. The large group of buildings on the right is one such resort, occupied by elegant shops and THE SCHOONERS INN, 207/967-5333, with a pricey, upscale restaurant serving northern Italian cuisine.

Beyond this last outpost of Kennebunkport's commerce, the road turns into ***Parsons' Way*** — an incredible gift of scenery for everyone's benefit. On the rocky ledges above the pounding surf are several well-placed benches for taking in the views of distant Wells Beach and Mount Agamenticus on the horizon. Further along the cape is a sidewalk for strolling in beautiful surroundings. If you happen to be at the tip of the cape just before high tide, you might see ***Blowing Cave***, where the waves catch a cleft in the rocks and spout up to thirty feet in the air.

On the inland side of the road is a stylish neighborhood of well-spaced summer cottages. As the road rounds the cape, look toward the impressive complex of houses on the rocky peninsula to the north, known as ***Walker's Point***. You may notice a number of plain cars with antennas on their roofs and people milling about — easy to understand once you realize that this is George Bush's summer cottage.

Opposite the entrance to Walker's Point is the large estate formerly owned by Kenneth Roberts, author of NORTHWEST PASSAGE and LYDIA BAILEY. The road passes through a neighborhood of newer homes overlooking the ocean, before coming to a stop sign. *Turn left, if you wish to return to the getting-and-spending of Dock Square.*

"In the autumn come deer to paddle in the salt water, and hulking moose . . . and turkeys occasionally; also teal, black ducks, and Canada geese in long lines and wedges; while always our orchards and alder runs are filled with woodcock and that toothsome but brainless bird, the partridge, who flies hastily into a tree at the approach of a barking dog, and stays there, befuddled, until the dog's owner walks up unnoticed and knocks him down." Kenneth Roberts, ARUNDEL.

To visit a tranquil, picture-book fishing village, *turn right. The road winds through a more modest part of Kennebunkport before catching up with rte. 9.* Continue for a short distance until you reach the tiny community of ***Cape Porpoise***. A sharp right will take you past some quaint New England houses, complete with lobster traps stacked up on their lawns. Many overlook the cove, full of lobster boats, with the ocean in the distance. *After about a mile the road ends, and you will have to retrace your route back to the village.*

While lobster buoys in each community have distinctive markings for identification, those at Cape Porpoise have traditionally been the most intricate. The harbor is so full of them that one yachtsman compared entering it to "trying to navigate a woodpile."

If you go straight, you will come to the "cape" at Cape Porpoise (actually, the town is composed of a group of islands). The only human activity at the end of the road centers on the fishing industry, as it has since the first settlers. For anyone hankering for some fried fresh fish, lobsters and steamers, MILLS ROAD LOBSTER POUND, 207/967-4607, is handy.

During Colonial days, Cape Porpoise rivaled Kennebunkport in the trading of dried fish and lumber for West Indian sugar, molasses, and rum.

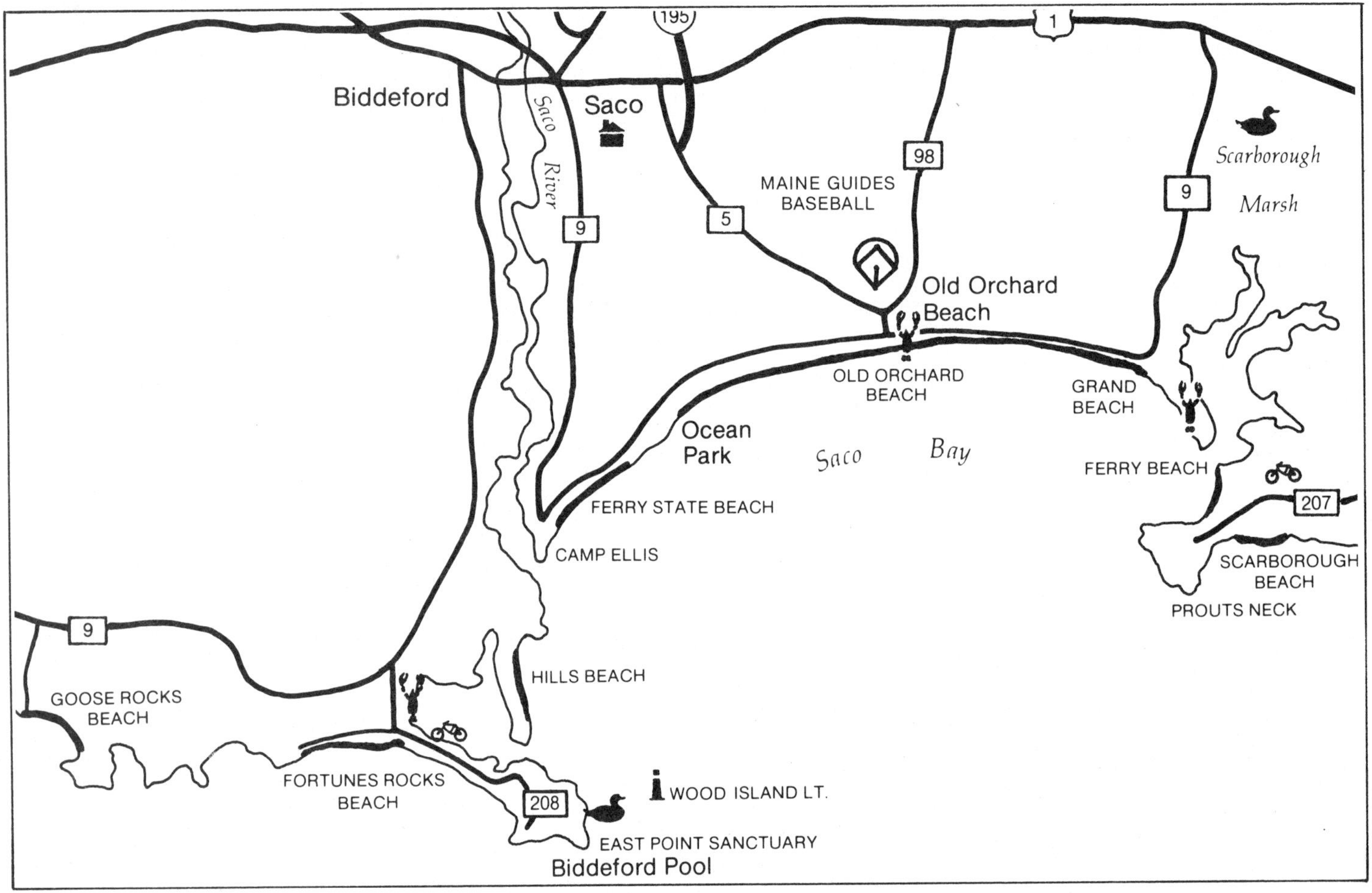

195
1
Biddeford
Saco
Saco River
9
5
98
9
MAINE GUIDES BASEBALL
Scarborough Marsh
Old Orchard Beach
OLD ORCHARD BEACH
GRAND BEACH
Ocean Park
Saco Bay
FERRY BEACH
FERRY STATE BEACH
CAMP ELLIS
207
SCARBOROUGH BEACH
PROUTS NECK
9
HILLS BEACH
GOOSE ROCKS BEACH
FORTUNES ROCKS BEACH
208
WOOD ISLAND LT.
EAST POINT SANCTUARY
Biddeford Pool

Commerce here today is a far cry from what it was in centuries past, but the fishing trade still represents an authentic way of life for a good part of the population along the coast.

After returning to the center of Cape Porpoise, head north on rte. 9. For a mile or so the road winds inland through a mixture of modest houses before passing through a sparsely populated section of good road.

Sidetrip: ***Goose Rocks Beach.*** Turn right onto Dyke Rd., opposite the group of large, old buildings with an unlikely clock tower topping them off. After traveling for about a mile through another section of the Rachel Carson Wildlife Refuge, you will arrive at Goose Rocks. This two-mile stretch of sand is uncrowded simply because it serves a small summer community, and parking is for residents only — another beach where it helps to be dropped off.

Rte. 9 becomes flat and wide as it continues north, with paved shoulders for easy biking. There are some lovely sights along the coast here, and we recommend that you *turn right when you reach the intersection of rte. 208, two and a half miles north of the Goose Rocks Rd.* Shortly after turning, you will see a sign on the right for ***Fortunes Rocks Beach***. This superb two-mile stretch of white sand also suffers (or benefits, depending upon your point of view) from a lack of parking. On the inland side of the road is Lily Pond, where migrating ducks are frequently spotted. *Returning to rte. 208, turn right toward the town of* ***Biddeford Pool***, one of the earliest settlements along this part of the coast.

"Biddeford Pool is a pleasing detour." Wallace Nutting, 1924.

The Pool.

In 1616 Sir Fernando Gorges sent explorers led by Richard Vines to this area; Vines made several trips along the coast before settling here at the mouth of the Saco River in the 1630s. Winter Harbor, as the first community along the northern edge of the Pool was known, attracted Englishmen looking for wealth in the new world but also willing to pay for land and fishing rights from the Indians. The early settlers lived here fairly tranquilly, until several drunken sailors tossed an Indian baby into the river to see if it was true that red men were born knowing how to swim. The infant — the son of Squando, a medicine man for the local tribe — died, and from that time on Indians made life incredibly difficult for the English. Not until 1746 was there any continual settlement of this part of the coast.

Today this lovely community remains part fishing village *(take the road on the left as you reach the bottom of the hill)*, and part prosperous year-round and summer cottage colony *(continue straight up the hill toward the ocean)*. At the tip of the peninsula is ***East Point Sanctuary***, a thirty-acre tract of fields, thickets, and pebble beaches managed by the Maine Audubon Society. *Level half-mile trail through sanctuary; no picnicking or other recreation permitted.*

The mudflats here offer some of the best birding in the region; best sighting time for shorebirds is an hour and a half before high tide. Look for migrating species, including snow buntings, in winter or shore birds in spring and fall, wading near the pool itself. Out at sea on ***Wood Island*** with its lighthouse, just north of the point, herons and egrets nest during the summer. *Returning to rte. 9, head north toward Saco and Biddeford.*

GREAT BLUE HERON

Sidetrip: ***Hills Beach.*** An alternate route is to turn right on Old Pool Road just before you reach rte. 9. This road, which parallels rte. 9, will take you to the beach. You will find excellent swimming on this one-third of a mile-long sand spit that protects a large tidal basin. When bathers and naturalists converge, however, parking can be tight. Old Pool Road continues north until it meets up with rte. 9.

An early explorer recounts an experience many sailors know all too well, as they try to navigate the waters between Cape Porpoise and Saco: ". . . before we could recover the harbour a great fog of mist took us [so] that we could not see a hundred yards from us. I perceiving the fog to come upon the Sea, called for a Compass and set the Cape land, by which we knew how to steer our course . . . no sooner done but we lost sight of land, and my other boat, and wind blew fresh against, so that we were enforced to strike sail and betake us to our Oars which we used with all the wit and strength we had, but by no means could we recover the shore that night. . . . At length I caused our Killick [a small anchor, perhaps even a stone] to be cast forth . . . which being done we commended ourselves to God by prayer . . . & put on a resolution to be as comfortable as we could . . ." Christopher Levett, 1628.

Rte. 9 turns inland, following the Saco River, which begins in the White Mountains and is popular with canoeists. The early settlers built so many mills along the river here that salmon soon deserted the Saco — much to the Indians' dismay. The Pepperrells of Kittery were quick to realize the potential here and bought land near the falls and an interest in the ferry across the river. In the 18th century the General Court of Massachusetts allowed colonists to hold a lottery, the proceeds of which went toward building the first of many bridges on the Saco.

Unfortunately, the intensive development that took place along the river in the 19th and 20th centuries has left little of this area's early history for visitors to see. *Continue along rte. 9 for about five miles before entering the mill town of* ***Biddeford***. The road is wide and straight, with little to distract the eye along the way.

From Sawmill to Condos.

Biddeford stands in contrast to any other town along this stretch of coast, for it was built, not on fishing or shipbuilding, but on textiles. The falls of the Saco River, seven miles inland from the Atlantic Ocean, made this site a natural one to locate mills so dependent on flowing water for their energy.

Even as early as 1662 there was a mill here — a sawmill erected by the son of John and Priscilla Alden. Lumber was long the principal trade along the Saco; clapboards, shingles, and laths were manufactured here. Then came textiles and the machines that made them. Today the near-vacant Pepperrell Mills dominate the landscape. All is not lost, however, for the buildings are being transformed for other uses.

Stay on rte. 9 and you will pass these impressive monuments to an industry departed for distant lands and cheap labor. The 30-acre island in the middle of the Saco River was first known as Indian Island, thickly forested and a natural fishing ground. In the 18th century, entrepreneur Thomas Cutts bought the island and set up a retail business in addition to shipbuilding and lumbering, and later an iron works that produced 3500 pounds of nails a day. By the 1820s most of the island was the site of a cotton factory.

Today you may see the beginnings of a new complex of condominiums, restaurants, and shops in this deserted group of factories: ***Saco Island***. This large development promises to be exciting not only because of the splendid site high above the river, but also because it offers a well-documented look into our industrial past. "Factory Island: Bricks, Mortar and Hope" (a series of exhibits, lectures, and videos cosponsored by the Dyer Library and the York Institute Museum) will elaborate on the history of textiles in Biddeford and Saco as well as the people — men, women, and children of New England, French-Canadian, Greek, and Scottish and New England heritage — who made these mills work. (Scheduled for fall 1987-1989).

As you're crossing the bridge to ***Saco***, you'll see J.R. FLANAGAN'S, 207/282-1617, a crisply stylish restaurant housed in an old brick building on the left. Interested in a seafood cocktail of smoked oysters, shrimp, and snow crab; quiche of the day, stir-fried selections, or scampi? This is a place to sample such fare.

As Saco's down-town buildings blend into huge turn-of-the-century and older homes, *rte. 9 takes a sharp right at the traffic light.* For those who have not had their fill of sand beaches, there are plenty along the coast here. But there are also more ahead. We recommend your heading straight through Saco to Scarborough's marsh and the rocky coast south of Portland.

Sidetrip: ***Camp Ellis.*** Turn right at the traffic light onto Beech St., rte. 9 east, for about four miles through a residential area to the signs for Camp Ellis Beach. This wonderfully funky community is falling into the ocean — and at all too rapid a pace. While there's not much beach here even at low tide, WORMWOOD'S SEAFOOD RESTAURANT, 207/282-9679, makes it worth the drive. You can get lobster any way you want here — boiled whole or two Maine (not South African) lobster tails, in stew, newburg, salad, on rolls, with or without stuffing — not to mention garlic shrimp and scallops, crab benedict, and creamy fish chowder.

Built on a prehistoric beach, Camp Ellis has always been a bit precarious, but lately the ocean has taken more sand than it's returned. Currently the shoreline is receding inland at a rate of almost two feet a year, and nothing — not the jetty that many blame for the erosion nor Saco's pouring thousands of dollars into saving the beach — seems able to stop it. One resident can list a dozen houses that have disappeared in the past twenty years; the beach has also lost 41 home lots in 80 years.

The sand the ocean is pulling away from Camp Ellis has stabilized the beaches at Old Orchard, Grand Beach, and Pine Point on the mouth of the Scarborough River. As one fisherman said, "Always nice to know that what used to hold up my house is going to hold up a condo at Old Orchard."

Sidetrip: ***Ferry Beach State Park***. Continue on rte. 9 to reach Ferry Beach. This well-developed park is popular because of the nearby summer colony and ample parking (fee). *Turn left on Ferry Rd., just past Baywood Colony on the right. In addition to the two and a half miles of fine sand, there are trails through the woods (look for the rare stand of tupelo trees along the banks of the Saco River), picnic tables, bathhouse, play areas.*

Sidetrip: ***Old Orchard Beach***, a large, well-known tourist attraction, offers much for those not afraid of being packed amidst sun worshipers and bathers. All told, there are seven miles of clean, white sand, a 490-foot pier, and a mammoth amusement park along the beach. Because of the carnival atmosphere, as well as the novelty shops, take-outs, motels, condominiums, and people, the area has aptly been called "Maine's Coney Island." If this is your style, you'll love Old Orchard Beach. For Canadians, it's nice to find, "On parle francais ici." *Fee parking. If you are coming from Ferry Beach, just continue on rte. 9 up the coast. From rte. 1, go east on rte. 5 to the beach. From the Maine Turnpike, get off at Exit 5 onto rte. 195, which will connect with rte. 5 to the beach.*

A 1905 photo shows Rose Kennedy, flanked by her father and father-in-law, clearly enjoying the sun and sand at Old Orchard Beach.

In the summer, Old Orchard Beach draws an average of 100,000 visitors WEEKLY!

Grand Beach and Pine Point. The condos stop north of Old Orchard, if you continue on rte. 9, and comfortable old beach homes reclaim your attention at Grand Beach. *Shortly after the sign for* ***West Scarborough****, rte. 9 veers sharply left or west. Head straight for Pine Point (don't turn onto rte. 9) at the mouth of the Scarboro River with its views of Prout's Neck.*

If you continue driving north, you'll come to PINE POINT FISHERMEN'S CO-OP, 207/883-3588, with lobster boats in the river and a deck for seafood take-out service. *Heading back on East Grande Ave. Ext., you'll hit rte. 9 west.*

If you choose to continue north on rte. 1 through Saco, Main St. passes large buildings on both sides. At one time these homes belonged to the mill owners; most of the workers lived on the other side of the river in Biddeford. Among these imposing homes was one built by J. G. Deering, Saco's leading 19th-century lumber magnate and philanthropist. Now the ***Dyer Library***, the building houses an impressive collection of Maine history and year-round exhibits. *Open Monday-Saturday. 371 Main Street, 207/282-3031.* Next door is the ***York Institute Museum***, which boasts an art gallery, period furnishings, and a colonial garden. *375 Main St., 207/282-3031. Open May-October; donation appreciated.*

Sidetrips for Kids: those traveling with youngsters may want to be on the lookout for several worthwhile commercial attractions along this strip of rte. 1:

- ***Maine Aquarium***, about 1.5 miles north of downtown Saco on the right, displays sharks, seals, eels, and other creatures of the deep. *Open daily year round; 207/284-4511. Admission or membership. Gift shop; refreshments and picnic facilities.*

• ***Aquaboggan Water Park***, another 1.5 miles further along rte. 1 on the left, is a good place for the whole family to cool off. *Open late June-Labor Day. Admission, refreshments. Huge water slide, pool, 18-hole miniature golf course, shuffleboard, and toddler's playground. 207/282-3112.*

Continue north from Saco on rte. 1 for approximately two more unspectacular miles to rte. 9 on the right. A mile and a half down this road is the next point of interest: ***Scarborough Marsh***, the largest salt marsh in Maine. The best way to enjoy this 3,000-acre wildlife sanctuary is to stop at the visitor center on the left to see what programs and events the Maine Audubon Society has in store.

Among the offerings are daily guided marsh walks, twice-weekly guided canoe trips, exhibits, slide shows, and lectures. Guided walks to the nearby beaches are offered, too. Or if you would rather be on your own to explore the teeming life of the salt marsh, rent a canoe and glide through the maze of waterways. *Visitor center free; open mid-June-Labor Day. Fees for guided tours and canoes.*

English naturalist John Jocelyn visited his brother in Scarborough in 1638 and found the company here both interesting and congenial, if somewhat rare. Visitors to the Jocelyn home regaled the English traveler with tales of sea mermen who oozed purple blood when their hands were cut off, a sea serpent "quoiled like a cable upon a rock", and a band of ghostly Indians who called a seaman by name from the shore at night, only to disappear when he appeared there the following morning. But what may have astounded Jocelyn the most was watching a certain Captain Wannerton quaff half a pint of beer in one swallow.

Trace your steps back to rte. 9 and continue along rte. 1 for another three miles to ***Scarborough.*** *Turn right onto rte. 207*; this road will lead you to the rocky shore that inspired Winslow Homer and to some of the area's best sand beaches. First comes ***Scarborough Beach State Park***, a well-developed park, with picnic tables, grills and a bathhouse. Known for its excellent surf, the beach itself is a wide, mile-long sandy barrier. It fronts on a freshwater pool, still known as Massacre Pond for the bloody battle settlers fought with the Indians here. *The fee parking lot is predictably full on hot days.*

Ferry Beach and ***Western Beach*** are also off rte. 207. These two beaches, separated by a rocky point for tidal pool exploration, are about a mile long combined. Western Beach is more sheltered, and

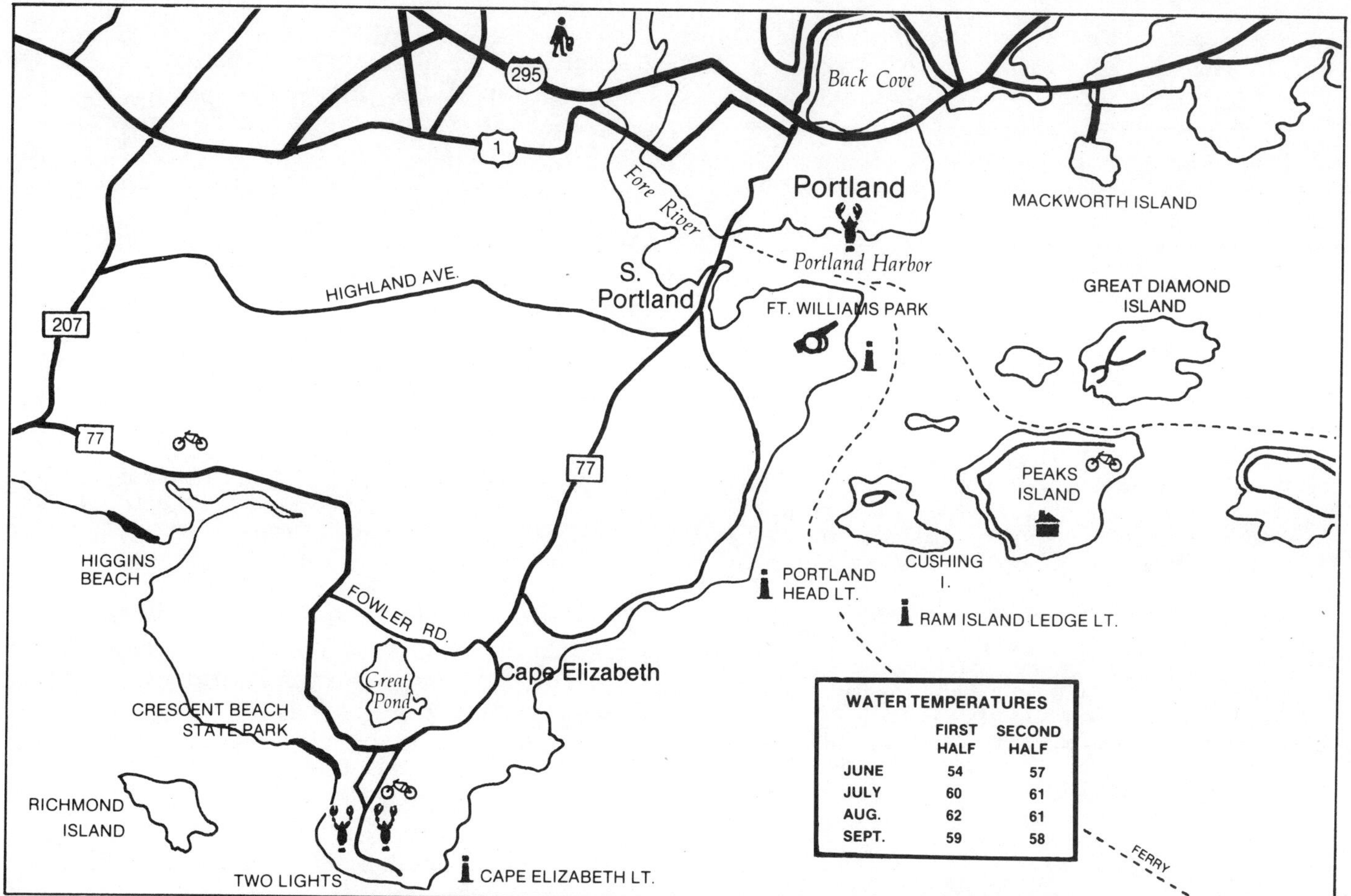

WATER TEMPERATURES

	FIRST HALF	SECOND HALF
JUNE	54	57
JULY	60	61
AUG.	62	61
SEPT.	59	58

has white sand, as well as a few low dunes. *Parking, if there is any, will be found at Ferry Beach.*

At the end of the road lies the lovely community of ***Prouts Neck***, made famous by artist Winslow Homer, who built his studio to overlook the crashing surf. Some of the artist's finest works — "The Fog Warning," "The Herring Net," "Eight Bells," "Winter Coast," "The Fox Hunt" — were painted here when this town was just a secluded fishing village. By the turn of the century, the Neck attracted more and more summer people, and the painter was forced to put a sign on his studio door, "Mr. Homer is not at home." *Most of the elegant residential area is closed to visitors, and parking is non-existent. It is best visited by bike.*

Local fisherman Henry Lee was the model for "The Fog Warning." One cold day when Homer began the sittings, he went to his well for a bucket of water and threw it on Lee to make him look more realistic. "You never heard such profanity in your life," one witness reported.

"Winslow's closes intimates were his pipe and brush," the pastor at St. James Chapel in Prout's Neck said of the artist. Homer lived alone, doing his own cooking except for a special meal which his neighbor Mrs. Seavey prepared every now and then. In old age, he came to resemble a sea captain, looking rather like a character in one of his own paintings. Although he had no patience with summer people criticising his work, Homer would allow his butcher to verbally tear his paintings to shreds. No doubt the painter would have been honored by the obituary the Scarborough postmaster wrote at his death in 1910: "He was a good man and a good citizen. If any man had a setback he was the first to help him. He was good to the poor. We shall miss him for a long time to come."

Returning from Prouts Neck on rte. 207, you will come to rte. 77 on the right that will lead you north. This is a pretty road, gently rolling, with a pleasing mixture of woods and open land. Pussy willows bloom along here in the spring, and it's a good biking route.

Sidetrip: ***Higgins Beach***. This old resort colony has an established feel about it. The cottages along this half-mile strip of sand are close together and comfortable, rather than impressive. *Take Ocean Ave. off rte. 77 to the right for Higgins Beach. Parking is limited.*

Continuing on rte. 77 will give you more marsh views and a good look at the Spurwink River to your right. About a mile past Ocean Ave. is the SPURWINK COUNTRY KITCHEN, 207/799-0006, one of our favorite old-fashioned restaurants. Pine paneling and tables, as well as down-East home cooking, mean an unpretentious atmosphere. You get your money's worth here — whether you're having baked beans or the lobster special (stew with a roll, sandwich, or salad). Pies and cakes are home-baked and taste as though they'd just won first prize at the county fair; there's even take-out service for picnics.

After crossing over the river and passing a pretty church and burying ground on the left, you'll see Fowler Rd., also on the left. If you're in a hurry, this is a short-cut to the other side of the peninsula. However, we recommend staying on rte. 77, a much more scenic drive. Further along you will come to the entrance to ***Crescent Beach State Park***.

In this well-developed park (picnic tables, snack bar) are two beaches: the eastern one is sandy for bathing, while the western one is stony and popular for ledge fishing. Among the unique natural features here are the harbor seals which can sometimes be seen sunning on the ledges of ***Richmond Island***, and the northernmost stand of wormwood in Maine. *Parking fee.*

From 1638 to 1648 Richmond Island was a substantial fishing community with about 50 dwellings, a corn mill, sheep and horses, plenty of arable land and trees. Today the island is low, flat, and bare — totally uninhabited.

Shortly after Crescent Beach is ***Two Lights State Park***. Named for its well-preserved lighthouses, this picturesque park is a combination of steep, rocky seascapes and inviting woodland trails. The views toward the Calendar Islands of Casco Bay are especially dramatic. *Picnicking. Parking fee.* Nearby TWO LIGHTS LOBSTER SHACK, 225 Two Lights Rd., 207/799-1677, has fried clams and lobster rolls. Open in season.

*Rte. 77 continues into residential **Cape Elizabeth**.* On the right is Ocean House Rd., a nice loop toward Prebbles and Trundy Points. The neighborhood is composed of older estates and more contemporary suburbia, but there are also plenty of sights if you simply *continue north on 77 to Shore Rd., just before the Mobil station.*

This road passes stands of birches, bogs, and impressive homes overlooking the water. Zeb Cove, a rocky beach on the right, has no parking. A couple of miles down Shore Road, you'll come to ***Fort Williams Park***, the former military installation at ***Portland Head Light***, another classic New England lighthouse where poet Henry Wadsworth Longfellow used to walk as a boy. *Picnic tables, facilities, paved paths for walking or jogging. Parking.*

*Continue along this shore route, past impressive homes, into **South Portland**, and its work-a-day* *neighborhoods, back to rte. 77.* Just before you cross the bridge into Portland, on the right you'll see the SNOW SQUALL RESTAURANT, 207/799-2232, the most popular seafood spot in the area. And for good reason! Pleasantly contemporary with the brick of walls and dark green of plants mirrored in table linens, this restaurant offers a wide variety of seafood. Cajun popcorn (as Louisiana crawfish is called) flown in regularly to Portland Airport, grilled swordfish, seafood brochette or linguine are delicious, as are the reasonably-priced wines and luscious pies.

The "Snow Squall" was a famous Casco Bay clipper ship in the China trade, but her finest hour may have come in 1863 when she became one of the few Union ships to outsail and escape the Confederate "Tuscaloosa." The next year, though, she ran aground.

The ship was rediscovered in 1979, and Portlanders have brought its bow home, where it will be displayed after careful preservation.

Maine's Biggest City.

Portland, the biggest city in the state and Maine's first capital, is small enough to find your way easily and seems relaxed in comparison to Boston or New York. Rush hour might slow you down for all of five minutes; I-295 makes travel here a snap. There are also excellent museums, music and performing arts, galleries, and restaurants without big city prices or hassles.

Portland's history is bound up with the water — Casco Bay (some of whose islands are part of the city itself), Portland Harbor, the Fore River, Back Cove, the Presumpscot River. The city was settled in 1631 and became a prosperous port until Indian raids in the late 17th century left it in ruins.

"Three miles from the open sea, sheltered by a bold rocky promontory and jewel-like islands, and situated on two hills close to the forest, is Portland, the first great American city to welcome the rising sun." Nathan Haskell Dole, 1928.

Shipping and shipbuilding revitalized the area before the American Revolution, when Portland became a center of anti-British sentiment. In 1775 the city was bombarded, and British shore parties set fire to what remained, leaving 2,000 colonists homeless, though hardly beaten. A decade after the shelling, Portland was on its feet again with new wharves and docks.

Steamboats and railroads meant new industry and prosperity in the 18th and 19th centuries, before another fire leveled most of the city in 1866. Although some 1800 buildings were destroyed then, Portland still retains a strong flavor of the past in carefully preserved homes and revitalized neighborhoods.

The Great Fire of July 4, 1866 was believed to have been started by a firecracker.

Today the city's importance is obvious. The commercial center of Maine, an important distribution point for northern New England, and a major oil port for Canada, Portland continues to grow with its glass towers, waterfront development, and attractive restorations. The longer you spend here, the more you'll come to appreciate this city.

"There are those who will tell you that as you sail out of Portland you finally have reached 'the real Maine' . . . a sailing paradise . . . The cool air is so clean that a city dweller's lungs want to burst with the marvel of it; the water is so clear you can see the lobsters scurry over the bottom; the winds rise on most days to take you on silent wings of canvas to new delights." Walter Cronkite, 1986.

As you continue on rte. 77 over the Fore River, you'll see the Portland International Ferry, a departure point for Nova Scotia. Further down the waterfront, there are numerous cruises into the bay, ferries to different islands, and charter boats for deep-sea fishing, sailing, or diving. *From the bridge, take any street running to the right to reach Commercial St. and the waterfront. If you're coming from I-95, take Exit 6A and follow I-295 to signs for the waterfront. All the sidetrips listed below depart from wharves along Commercial St.*

Sidetrip: ***Yarmouth, Nova Scotia***. Prince of Fundy Cruises cuts off 600 miles of driving. *Reservations advised for nightly departures with cabins for the 10-hour ferry trip. P.O. Box 4216, Station A, Portland 04101, 207/775-5616. Dining facilities; private cabins.*

Sidetrip: ***Casco Bay Lines***, Custom House Wharf, 207/774-7871, has frequent trips to islands throughout the bay:

The closest stop from Portland, ***Peaks Island*** (whose 1,500 year-round population swells to 6,000 in season) has been called the "little city in the bay." Its Civil War Museum is open daily in the summer. *17-minute ferry ride departs almost hourly. Be advised that you may have a several-hour wait with a car returning to the mainland; taxis meet each ferry on Peaks. Peaks Island*

Peaks Island's proximity to the mainland, an advantage today, was a real liability for early settlers in the Portland area, who were frequently attacked by Indians summering on the island.

By the beginning of this century, Peaks was well known to tourists who came by steamer from New York or Boston and by the Grand Trunk Railway from Canada. For 25 cents you could buy a round-trip ferry ticket from Portland to this island with its theatres, shooting gallery, ferris wheel, wild animals, daily balloon ascensions, and roller rinks.

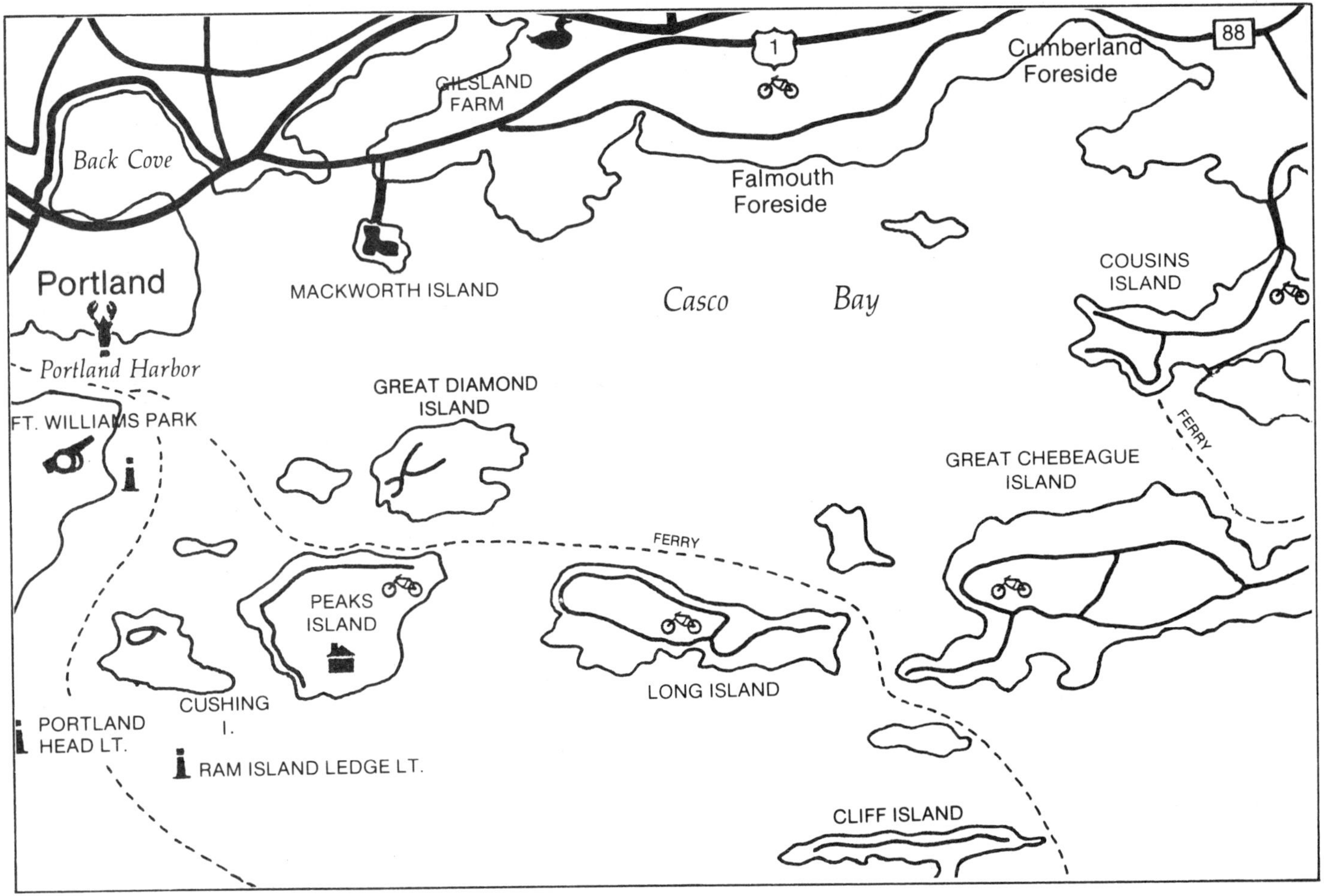
88
1
Cumberland Foreside
GILSLAND FARM
Back Cove
Falmouth Foreside
Portland
MACKWORTH ISLAND
Casco Bay
COUSINS ISLAND
Portland Harbor
GREAT DIAMOND ISLAND
FT. WILLIAMS PARK
FERRY
GREAT CHEBEAGUE ISLAND
FERRY
PEAKS ISLAND
LONG ISLAND
CUSHING I.
PORTLAND HEAD LT.
RAM ISLAND LEDGE LT.
CLIFF ISLAND

also has an inn (THE MOONSHELL), restaurants, beaches, gift shop, bike rentals. Bikers will enjoy ***Long Island***, three miles long and a mile wide; Big Sandy Beach is popular with Portlanders. *No beach facilities; you may want to use rest rooms on the ferry. The island has a restaurant, convenience store, and gift shop.*

Big Sandy Beach is sometimes called "Singing Beach" because the waves make an eerie sound when the wind is right.

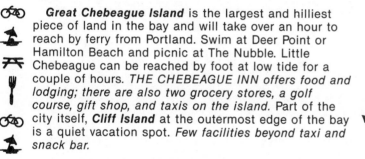

Great Chebeague Island is the largest and hilliest piece of land in the bay and will take over an hour to reach by ferry from Portland. Swim at Deer Point or Hamilton Beach and picnic at The Nubble. Little Chebeague can be reached by foot at low tide for a couple of hours. *THE CHEBEAGUE INN offers food and lodging; there are also two grocery stores, a golf course, gift shop, and taxis on the island.* Part of the city itself, ***Cliff Island*** at the outermost edge of the bay is a quiet vacation spot. *Few facilities beyond taxi and snack bar.*

The Abenakis were the first summer people on Chebeague Island, and Indians have come back for centuries since. The Passamaquoddys used to hunt seals here. In the 1930s, one Indian family used to pitch their tent near the tennis courts, selling baskets and moccasins to visitors.

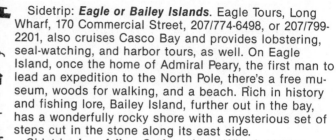

Sidetrip: ***Eagle or Bailey Islands***. Eagle Tours, Long Wharf, 170 Commercial Street, 207/774-6498, or 207/799-2201, also cruises Casco Bay and provides lobstering, seal-watching, and harbor tours, as well. On Eagle Island, once the home of Admiral Peary, the first man to lead an expedition to the North Pole, there's a free museum, woods for walking, and a beach. Rich in history and fishing lore, Bailey Island, further out in the bay, has a wonderfully rocky shore with a mysterious set of steps cut in the stone along its east side.

Sidetrip: ***Longfellow Cruises***, Long Wharf, 207/774-3578, has narrated trips that focus on lobstering, lighthouses, and shipwrecks in these waters. *Snack bar.*

Captain Kidd is said to have buried treasure on Jewell's Island in Casco Bay; legends of pirate gold and smuggling refer to Orr's, Bailey's, and Haskell's Islands as well. In 1840 a resident of Bailey's Island actually did find a pot of buried gold, while he was out duck hunting.

Sidetrip: ***Buccaneer Lines***, Long Wharf, 207/799-8188, offers hour and longer cruises of the bay, including a tour of ***House Island*** with its Civil War Fort Scammel and a lobster cookout.

Hog Island is the site of Fort Gorges, built in 1857 under the direction of then Secretary of War Jefferson Davis (later the President of the Confederacy). House Island may have been the first island Christopher Levett occupied in 1623 and where he left ten men, promising to return for them but never doing so.

After crossing the bridge from South Portland, continue on rte. 77, past the Captain Nathaniel Dyer House on the right, but don't turn left at the light. Stay on York St. instead through the commercial section and head for the old port district. York St. runs into Pleasant St., which quickly becomes Fore St. The large parking garage on your left is a good place to start your exploration of this interesting city. Unfortunately, others may have beaten you to it, as the Fore St. garage is often full. *If so, go back a half block and turn down the hill on Union Street for an alternate garage, which closes early in the evening.*

Old Port Exchange.

This Victorian reconstruction of Portland's waterfront is one of the most vital parts of the modern city. Period architecture, cobblestone streets, brick sidewalks, old gas lamps meld into modern galleries, tromp d'oeil murals, up-scale shops and restaurants. If you're hungry, try THE BLUE MOON CAFE, 425 Fore St. right next to the garage, 207/871-0663. This sleek, art-deco restaurant offers interesting dishes (baby Brie stuffed with fresh crab, pesto chicken salad in a crisp taco "bowl," fresh catch of the day) at reasonable prices — and live jazz in the evenings.

Across the street, THE BAKER'S TABLE, 434 Fore St., 207/775-0303, is popular for brunch and may have the best desserts around. A couple of blocks down the street, THE SEAMEN'S CLUB, 375 Fore St., 207/772-7311 is a real favorite. Built just after the Great Fire of 1866, the restaurant is a landmark with its Gothic windows and medallions carved in wood. And its food is equal to its facade. The club offers some of the finest seafood anywhere. Grilled salmon steak, finnan haddie, cioppino compete here with New England specialities, like the hot turkey sandwich with a sherried dill sauce. An actual seamen's club in the 1940s, the interior is today an eclectic amalgamation of brick, Turkish saddlebags, sailing prints and old books.

As you wander through the shops and galleries of Old Port Exchange, there are many other fine

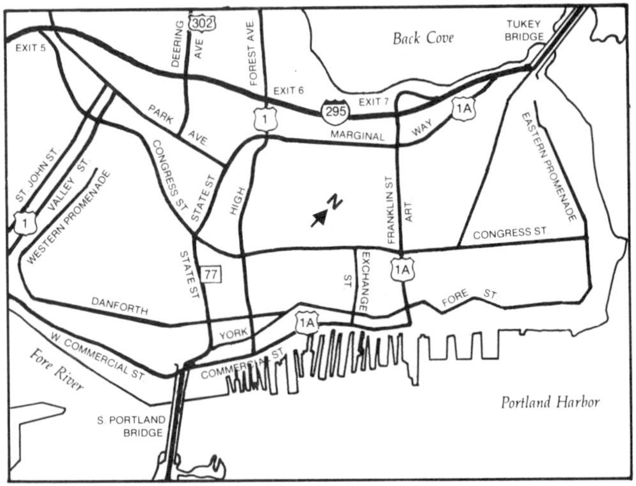

DOWNTOWN PORTLAND

restaurants to sample. We can recommend RAPHAEL'S, 36 Market St., 207/773-4500, Portland's most popular newcomer. A raw bar and Italian cuisine make a wonderful combination, whether you're dining formally upstairs or in the trendy lounge below. F. PARKER REIDY'S, 83 Exchange Street, 207/773-4731, is another restaurant that makes the most of its historic setting. Tile floors and mahogany create a well-heeled atmosphere; fresh fish (blackened or broiled) and steaks are specialities.

For a sandwich or light meal and a great bar, try DOCK FORE, 336 Fore St., 207/772-8619. And you don't need to have kids with you to enjoy BEN AND JERRY'S, 97 Exchange St., 207/773-3222. There's no place like this on a hot day for fresh fruit sherbet or one of their incredible floats.

Dining Out in Portland.

Other dining spots of note in the city include: CAFE ALWAYS, 47 Middle St., 207/774-9399, offers the kind of ethnic flavor — from Creole to Thai — that enlivens any port. HAMILTON'S INDIA RESTAURANT, nearby at 43 Middle St., 207/773-4498 is another exotic restaurant favored by Portlanders. For cooking from all parts of Italy, try MARIA'S at 337 Cumberland Ave., 207/772-6957, or THE ROMA, 769 Congress St., 207/773-9873 for a romantic dinner.

For a bite to eat at the Performing Arts Center, there's the MADD APPLE CAFE, 23 Forest Ave., 207/774-9698, with reasonably-priced New Orleans cuisine. THE GOOD EGG CAFE, 705 Congress St., 207/773-0801, continues to win, hands down, for the best breakfast, although the wait can be long in this tiny hole-in-the-wall. Once you're seated, strong coffee is guaranteed to wake you up — if loud rock music hasn't already. But breakfast here is worth the wait. Besides homemade muffins, French toast, or pancakes, there are "good eggs" on corned beef hash, scrambled eggs with a variety of toppings served in pita bread, or smoked salmon and cream cheese with your eggs.

Henry Wadsworth Longfellow found Portland's waterfront fascinating:

"I remember the black wharves and the slips,
And the sea-tides tossing free;
And Spanish sailors with bearded lips,
And the beauty and mystery of the ships,
And the magic of the sea."

The young-at-heart will get a kick out of eating at DiMILLO'S floating restaurant on Long Wharf, 207/772-2216. This converted ferry offers seafood and Italian dishes as well as a chance to watch what's going on along Portland's busy waterfront. But the best views of the harbor and the city can be enjoyed along with well-prepared, reasonably priced food at CHANNEL CROSSING, 231 Front St., across the harbor in South Portland, 207/799-

5552. Steak benedict and the grilled lobster sandwich are tasty lunch-time specialties; the chocolate truffle with raspberry sauce is always divine!

The Arts Are Alive and Well in Portland.

Try to take time to sample some of the city's cultural wealth. In addition to the attractive galleries that offer paintings, sculpture, photography, or fabric art for sale, there are important exhibits here. ***The Portland Museum of Art***, 7 Congress Sq., 207/775-6148, is a good place to start. I. M. Pei's design incorporates local brick and granite into a startling post-modern structure that houses the Charles S. Payson collection of 19th- and 20th-century work. (The paintings of Winslow Homer and Andrew Wyeth capture the special beauty of this area.) Early American and Federal period furnishings and decorative art, an extensive collection of glass (including Portland glass), silver, and ceramics round out the permanent exhibit.

> Charles Shipman Payson, a Maine boy who made good, donated over $23 million to the Portland Museum of Art. Besides his career as an industrialist with interests in railroads, steel, oil, and uranium, he was also a backer of America's Cup yachts and a horse breeder.

Connoisseurs consider the ***Joan Whitney Payson Gallery of Art*** at Westbrook College, 716 Stevens Avenue, 207/797-9546, to be a small jewel in Portland's cultural crown. A modern box of a building on the Westbrook College campus, this tiny museum is worth the drive. The permanent collection, displayed each summer, includes at least one work each by the likes of Chagall, Degas, Picasso, Renoir, Sargent, Van Gogh. *From I-295 take Exit 6B (Forest Ave. north) and follow the signs for rte. 302 or Forest Avenue. You'll pass through a busy commercial area (be aware that you need to bear right to stay on rte. 302 at the traffic light before Dunkin' Donuts) until you come to a wooded area on your left (Baxter Woods). At the next traffic light, turn left onto Walton Ave. Then take a right at the stop light onto Stevens Ave., and you'll soon see Westbrook College on your left. Turn left on College St. and drive all the way to the end, jogging left behind the library.*

From downtown or the Old Port Exchange: take the Franklin St. Arterial to Marginal Way. Turn left onto Marginal Way; then right onto Forest Ave. Go approximately two miles to Rte. 9, and turn left. At the stop sign, turn right onto Stevens Ave. and follow directions above the rest of the way.

The Gallery appreciates donations.

Part owner of art galleries in Long Island and Palm Beach, Joan Whitney Payson frequently loaned works to exhibitions or friends. In the 1960s she asked her son, John, to choose the paintings in her collection that most impressed him; those works constitute the core of the Westbrook collection.

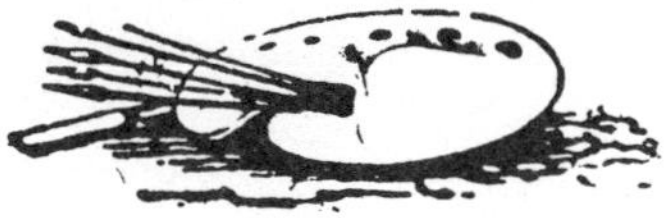

For music lovers, there's the ***Portland Symphony Orchestra***, 62 years old and going strong under newly-appointed conductor Toshi Shimada. *Classical, pops, and candlelight concerts; call 207/773-8191 for information and prices*. Summer visitors can join residents for free concerts at noon and early evening (check local papers for performances). ***The Portland Concert Association*** (207/772-8630) brings nationally acclaimed musicians and dancers here, while the ***Portland Lyric Theatre*** (207/799-1421) presents three fully-staged Broadway musicals, fall through spring, in a renovated church.

Portland Stage Company puts on six productions of established and new plays each season (again, fall through spring) at the Performing Arts Center, 25-A Forest Ave., 207/774-1043. A similar schedule holds for the area's oldest community theatre group, ***Portland Players***, 207/799-7337, but even if you're here only in the summer, you CAN enjoy professional performances at ***Maine Theatre*** June through August. Westbrook College's company-in-residence produces three separate plays at Waynflete School, Wednesdays-Sundays, 207/871-7101. There are also two local modern dance companies with performances throughout the year: ***Casco Bay Movers*** (207/871-1013) and ***Ram Island Dance Company*** (207/773-2562).

Kid's Stuff.

There's even a professional company that produces musical and theatrical entertainment just for kids. The ***Children's Theatre of Maine*** puts on original and traditional works; performances at Luther Bonney Auditorium on the Portland campus of The University of Southern Maine, 207/774-9481. Nearby in the Science Building, 96 Falmouth St., is ***Southworth Planetarium*** with its projector shows of the sky. *Sunday, Wednesday, Friday at 7:30 pm; reservations suggested. 207/780-4249.*

Cumberland County Civic Center, 207/775-3458, offers events the whole family can enjoy — like the Ice Capades — and is home to the Maine Mariners, an American Hockey League team. Then there's the ***Children's Museum of Maine***, 746 Stevens Ave., 207/797-KITE. Located near the entrance to the Payson Gallery on the Westbrook College campus, this museum is a three-story house where each room gives children a different idea or theme to explore. A working switchboard in one allows small-fry to call other rooms, an old-fashioned cash register rings up pre-computer-age purchases, ''feely'' boxes encourage sensory exploration, Snug Harbor has a pirate's den and a ship's wheel to steer. *Open daily plus one evening a week in the summer; enrichment programs for the whole family. Membership or admission.*

Across the street is the ***Children's Resource Center***, 207/797-0525, where recycled industrial products — dowels, buttons, shoelaces, colored wax, zippers, bottle caps, foam rubber of various sizes, scraps of fabric, wood, or leather — beckon to young, creative minds, and at prices even a kid can afford. *Open year-round. Follow directions to Payson Gallery, page 62. Museum and center are just beyond Westbrook College campus.*

When you're in the Old Port area, there's a wonderful children's bookstore, The Enchanted Forest at 377 Fore St., 207/773-8651. Whether you're looking for paperbacks to keep the kids busy on the trip home or classics to last a lifetime, this store will have the books you want — and toys to keep the little ones amused while you browse.

The Portland Observatory, 138 Congress St., a barn-red, shingled watchtower built in 1807, is always fun for children; family programs on local history and sea lore are special features here in the summer. *Nominal fee.* Greater Portland Landmarks, Inc., 165 State St., 207/774-5561, which sponsors the series at the Observatory, provides educational walking tours of the city for school groups, as well as special boat tours of Portland Harbor and islands in Casco Bay that are great family outings.

PORTLAND OBSERVATORY

Built as a lookout for ships, the Portland Observatory played an important role in bringing the Grand Trunk Railroad here. In the 19th century, Boston and Portland vied for Canadian trade, much the way they do today. A lookout from the top of the observatory spied the mail boat from Montreal and signaled a packet in the harbor to speed the mail to stage-drivers Hobbs, Bodge, and Waterhouse. They then covered the 300 miles left in twenty hours at an average speed of 15 miles an hour. Such efforts opened Canadian eyes to the advantages of Portland Harbor.

Exploring Portland's Past.

Despite major fires, there remain many fascinating old buildings here, some juxtaposed to handsome modern ones. Probably the best way to get to know this city is through a series of walking tours, sponsored by Greater Portland Landmarks above. *Guided tours last one to one-and-a-half hours; $2.50 a person for groups of ten. Or you can purchase printed tours to take at your own pace for just pennies apiece.* For those who prefer to ride, but would rather not worry about parking, Landmarks also offers bus tours, called "Step-On Guides." *Groups pay $35 per guide.*

> The 1866 fire devastated 200 acres in Portland — destroying every newspaper, most banks, almost all the churches and public buildings — with property losses soaring to $10,000,000.

Besides their booklet on the Old Port Exchange, Greater Portland Landmarks has three other self-guided tours: Congress St., State St., and the Western Promenade.

• ***Congress St.***, the transportation and commercial spine of this peninsula, has an interesting history that pre-dates the Revolution and continues into contemporary buildings. The tour begins at the Romanesque Revival library (now the Portland School of Art), which was given to the city in the late 19th century by philanthropist and former mayor James Baxter, and ends at Munjoy Hill, a point 160 feet above sea level, near Eastern Cemetery. En route you'll see the Charles Q. Clapp block with one of the two remaining "flatiron" buildings in the city; the First Parish Church, the first major granite building here with an antique weathervane from the original "Old Jerusalem" meetinghouse; and the stunningly modern Portland Public Library.

PORTLAND LIBRARY

This tour also includes the ***Wadsworth-Longfellow House***, 487 Congress St., 207/774-1822. *Open June - mid-October, Tuesdays - Saturdays; admission. Adjacent garden is open year-round; free.* The first brick home in Portland and the oldest remaining residence on this peninsula, the original colonial structure was begun shortly after the city's bombardment by the British. General Peleg Wadsworth had bricks shipped from Philadelphia, although a fire in 1814 destroyed the original gable roof. The third story and Federal-style hip roof were added later; you can still see a difference in the brickwork. This was home to Henry Wadsworth Longfellow who lived here until 1843. His first wife died in this house, and the poet's grief inspired THE RAINY DAY.

The Maine Historical Society, next door at 485 Congress St., 207/774-1822, maintains a library with the state's largest collection of town, church, family, and commercial histories, as well as a museum. *Open Tuesdays, Wednesdays, and Fridays; year round.* Another landmark in the area is the ***Neal Dow Memorial***, 714 Congress St., 207/773-7773. *Open year round, Mondays - Saturdays, 11 am - 4 pm. Free.* A Quaker by birth, Dow was an early activist for women's rights, abolition of slavery, prison reform, and temperance. His Federal-style mansion today houses family silver, china, furnishings, and paintings as well as papers and memorabilia from Dow's political and military careers.

Portlander Dow helped organize the Maine Temperance Union in 1838 and drafted the famous "Maine Law" legislating Prohibition here. As mayor, though, he had difficulty enforcing his own law.

• The next neighborhood to tour, ***State St.***, gives visitors a glimpse into 18th century Portland. Joseph Holt Ingraham, a local silversmith, was responsible for development here, buying up an entire tract of land from the crest of the hill down to the waterfront. He built himself an imposing home at 51 State St. before selling off lots to others. Architecture in this area reflects the elaborate early Federal style as well as the more conservative structures from the Embargo of 1807, Greek Revival from Portland's heyday as state capital, followed by Italianate and Victorian designs. Some of the more interesting sights along the way include: Franklin Simmons' statue, dedicated to Longfellow; the Richard Hunnewell House, at 156 State St., designed by Alexander Parris with additions by John Calvin Stevens; the Elihu Deering House, 79 High St., built by a Portland carver who became a leading merchant; and Park Street Row, a group of twenty townhouses surrounded on three sides by a common park.

The Embargo hit Portland particularly hard, producing shipping and trade losses in excess of a million dollars. By the time the bill was repealed in 1809, sixty percent of seacoast residents were unemployed, and soup kitchens dotted the city.

The Ruggles Sylvester Morse House, commonly known as ***The Victoria Mansion***, 109 Danforth St. between State and High Sts., 207/772-4841, is considered "one of the finest examples of 19th-century eclectic architecture to survive in the United States.'' New Haven architect Henry Austin designed this Italian villa for Morse, a Mainer who made his fortune in New Orleans. Interior frescoes, canvas insets, and elaborate woodwork make this home unusual. *Open in the summer; admission, group rates.*

Despite considerable abolitionist sentiment in Maine, many Portland merchants felt ambivalent at the outbreak of the Civil War. Much of the city's trade centered around cotton, and it was not unusual for a successful merchant to keep a home in New Orleans as well as Portland.

After the Confederate raider ''Alabama'' captured eleven Maine-built vessels during the war, rebel Navy Lt. Charles W. Read grew bold enough to venture into Portland Harbor, transferring his men from one captured vessel to another. Merchants or not, Portlanders must have been delighted when their own makeshift naval force finally captured Read.

• An early attempt at civic improvement, the ***Western Promenade*** is another tour you might like to take in Portland. When the first Europeans settled here, what is today a neighborhood of huge homes was heavily wooded with a sizeable swamp. In the late 18th century, wealthy merchant William Vaughan built here, hoping to encourage others to do the same and thereby increase the value of his own property. But he was forced to sell his holdings during the Embargo. Then in 1836 Mayor James Baxter incorporated the Promenade into the Olmstead plan for city parks. It provided residents with a place to walk, picnic, or shoot birds.

As late as 1745, the woods were so thick in what is now the Western Promenade that the inhabitants of Falmouth Neck (as Portland was known until 1786) felt compelled to clear the land, lest it provide cover for Indian attacks.

But The Great Portland Fire of 1866 had more to do with development of the Western Promenade than any plans the developers or officials might have made. Virtually overnight new streets and homes sprang up, widely spaced to prevent flames from leaping from one to another. The city's leading 19th-century capitalist, John Bundy Brown, built perhaps the most imposing residence, ''Bramhall,'' named for the hill itself. Although ''Bramhall'' has since been torn down, you can still get a sense of how big this property was by looking at those that remain on its site, 147-163 Western Promenade. Brown's estate extended east and west between the Promenade and Vaughan Sts., north and south between Bowdoin and Pine Sts.

Constructed with the profits from Brown's success in real estate and his sugar refinery down on the waterfront, ''Bramhall'' boasted an important painting and sculpture collection.

Except for the William Vaughan House, 387 Danforth St., a wooden Federal structure that precedes other homes here by at least 50 years, most of the buildings in the Promenade reflect the influence of architects Francis Fassett or John Calvin Stevens. Bowdoin St. shows Stevens' work most clearly with shingle style and gambrel roofs, incorporating early New England architecture into turn-of-the-century styles. Fassett's high Victorian Gothic fantasies remain for all to admire in the Williston Congregational Church, 32 Thomas St., and the Centennial duplex, that he built for himself and his son at 117-119 Pine St. Using brick, free-stone, slate, wood, and iron within a consistently vertical framework, Fassett recreated the feeling of the Middle Ages right here in New England.

Throughout the Promenade area, Queen Anne, Swiss style, Gothic revival, "stick" style, second Renaissance revival, and colonial revival mingle with Italianate homes. The Harrison Bird Brown House at 400 Danforth St. is an example of the latter. The best known Portland painter of the 19th century, Brown worked in a studio attached to this house.

A painter of the Hudson River and Luminist schools of American art, Brown dramatically captured the coast in his work.

The ***Stroudwater*** section of Portland is also interesting and easily reached by car from I-295. *Take the Congress St. exit and follow signs to rte. 22 west through a commercial/residential area (past the Ramada Inn, Westgate Shopping Center, and the airport). Turn left onto Westbrook St. at the light just past the water; the village is on the right.*

In its early days, Portland was an island, separated from the mainland by a stream from the Fore River to Back Cove.

The Tate House, an elegant colonial home, 1270 Westbrook St., 207/774-9781, was built in 1755 by a local mast agent. Still unpainted, it boasts an unusual window treatment of its gambrel roof. Fine paneling downstairs, original timbers of post-and-beam construction, and a center chimney with eight fireplaces make it an interesting contrast to most Portland homes. *Open May 15 - October 15, closed Mondays and holidays; admission.* Across Congress St. (rte. 9) on Westbrook St. is the Stroudwater Burying Ground, with a stone from 1739 and many unmarked graves.

Portland is difficult to leave, but there's much more to see and do before you head home. North of the city the coast becomes even rockier, sand beaches all but disappear, and pine trees dominate the landscape. *Of the three routes north, we recom-*

mend I-295 to rte. 1 (Exit 9, Falmouth Foreside).

After crossing over the river, look for Baxter School Rd., the third right which will lead you to ***Mackworth Island***, one of the few Calendar Islands that can be reached by car. Today it is the site of a school for the deaf; however, there is a nice path around the island, popular with Portlanders. *Very limited parking. About a mile after you cross the Presumpscot River bridge, rte. 88 veers off to the right.*

The Presumpscot.

Before turning onto rte. 88, you might want to visit ***Gilsland Farm***, headquarters of the Maine Audubon Society. This 70-acre tract of woods, fields, and salt marshes along the Presumpscot River offers, in just one location, almost all the diversity found in Maine. *An extensive self-guided trail runs through the sanctuary; free. Bookstore, information, rest room facilities; special programs for families year-round. 207/781-2330.*

The Audubon Society is justifiably proud of its modern headquarters — the largest solar-heated building in the state. An old center-chimney cape, on your right as you enter the sanctuary, has been retrofitted for solar heating, and you are welcome to examine it on a self-guided tour.

To get to the sanctuary, look for the old access road that angles off to the left 0.8 mile after the Presumpscot River bridge. The road is opposite a sign on the right side of rte. 1 that says "Bramhall

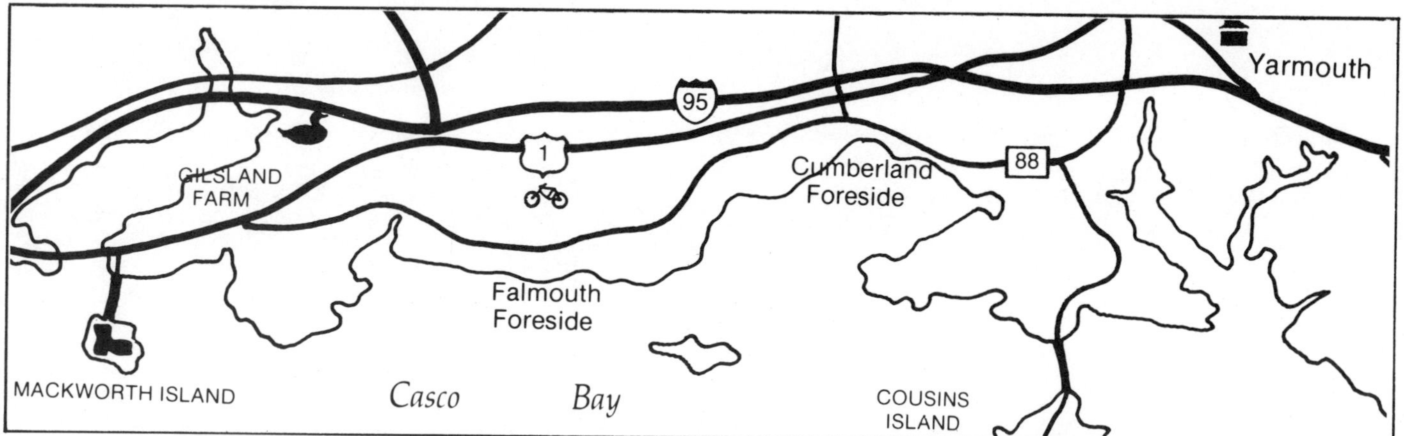

Field." After turning onto the access road, you will see the Gilsland Farm sign, leading you into the sanctuary.

Rte. 88 winds its way through a prosperous residential area, ***Falmouth Foreside***, with some of the prettiest homes anywhere in New England. Many waterfront estates have breathtaking views of Casco Bay and the islands. The only thing missing is any sign of commercial activity.

If you're hungry, look for THE GALLEY RESTAURANT at Handy Boat Landing, 207/781-4262, on your right. The islands in Casco Bay can be seen from the dining rooms and lounge, and have also been reflected in the menu: both haddock and chicken dinners are named for different islands. Whaleboat Island means sour cream and mushroom topping, while Sturdivant Island is an elaborate spinach, crab, onion, wine, and cheese concoction. You can also get Maine lobster clambake or a generous Sunday brunch here. Both the boat landing and the Portland Yacht Club next door take advantage of a large anchorage. In August you can watch the Monhegan Race for ocean-going yachts here.

The same up-scale neighborhood continues into ***Cumberland Foreside***, another place to catch a ferry with a much shorter ride over to ***Great Chebeague Island***. The water taxi from Cousins Island is not equipped for cars, and parking at the dock is very limited. Motorists must park at Cumberland School, four miles inland, and ride a bus to the ferry. *To find the school, take exit 9 off I-95 and follow rte. 1 north three miles to Tuttle Rd. Turn inland and head northwest two and three-quarters miles to Drowne Rd. and the Cumberland Elementary School. Contact Chebeague Transportation Company, 207/846-3700 for a schedule; fee.*

Chebeague Islanders used to make their living carrying granite in "stone sloops" from New England quarries to ports like Boston, New York, and Philadelphia.

SLOOP

Sidetrip: ***Cousins Island.*** Further on rte. 88 is a sign indicating the road to Cousins Island. If you turn right here, you will cross a bridge onto the island; immediately on your left is an uncrowded beach along the bay, always warmer for swimming than the ocean. The only problem is the insistent power line above, lessening the beauty of this spot. Bikers heading for the ferry should continue straight ahead until you see the sign "To Chebeague Island" on your right; turn left onto Wharf Rd. and go all the way to the end. *The water taxi takes only 15 minutes to reach the island; fee. See page 59 for details on Great Chebeague.*

For close to 200 years, fishermen of Casco Bay sought out a certain spring on Cousins Island that bubbles up about a foot at low tide and is said to ensure longevity for those who drink it. Chemical analysis proved the water from the spring to be rich in iron.

Yarmouth.

Rte. 88 eventually runs under rte. 1 and I-95, ending up in the bustling, but charming village of ***Yarmouth***. Twice destroyed by Indians, the town survived to become a shipbuilding center; over 300 seafaring vessels were built here in the 19th century. Sailing, an annual clam festival (held the third weekend in July), and the town's colonial flavor make it popular with tourists and as a place to live.

Although women were taboo aboard early sailing vessels, by the late 19th century Yarmouth sea captains' wives routinely shipped out with their husbands. Ship owners found captains who sailed with their families took better care of their craft and were less likely to spend money on hotels when in port. In fact, so many women along the coast followed their men to sea that the State of Maine passed an education law that paid them a teacher's wage, if they taught their children lessons aboard ship.

You may notice several old burying grounds on the right side of rte. 88 past the ''Historic Yarmouth'' sign. Ledge Cemetery, rte. 88 and Gilman Rd., is a well-maintained ground that dates from 1770. A brief walk ahead will take you to the oldest graveyard, Pioneers' Burial Ground, where Indian fighters and early settlers rest quietly.

Yarmouth was founded in 1631, but Indian raids threatened the settlement with its life in 1684, attacking colonists while they were building a stockade here. One of the town's founders, Walter Gendell, heard the attack and supposedly seized a keg of gun powder, bribing a black man to row him to the fort. While he successfully turned the tide in that battle, the Indians returned several weeks later, killing and torturing any settlers who had not fled to Jewell's Island.

Follow rte. 88 into town, turning west on rte. 115, up the hill to Yarmouth. CAMP HAMMOND, 74 Main St., 207/846-3895, set back on your right behind the gas station, still maintains a turn-of-the-century atmosphere. Built in 1888 by George Hammond, part owner of Yarmouth's Forest Paper Co., this huge home has changed little. Its ''mill construction,'' a solid-wall building technique, was considered protection against fire, mice, and insects. The grounds were landscaped by Frederick Law Olmsted, who designed New York's Central Park and Boston's Fenway.

The Grand Trunk Railroad Station, across the street, has found a new life as a florist shop. And you'll find antique and craft shops in old buildings along Main St.

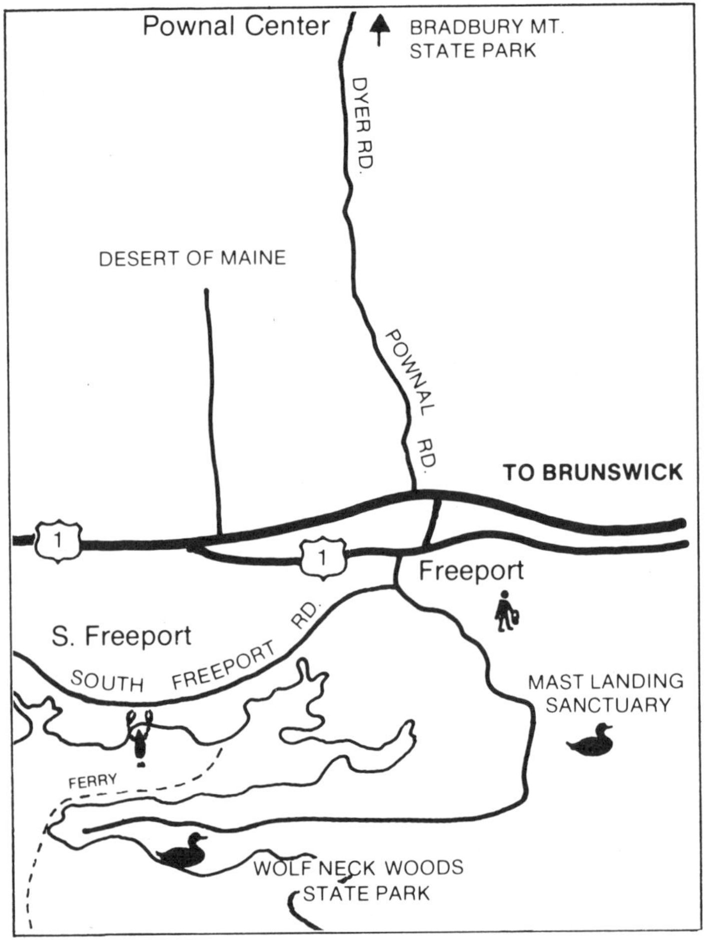

If you're just ready to stretch your legs, West Elm St. is a pretty residential walk. ***The Meeting House***, restored by the Village Improvement Society, is down the first road to your right. *Open one afternoon a week in the summer; free. Call 207/846-6259 for information.*

Or you might enjoy a walk along the ***Royal River***. *If so, turn right from Main St. (rte. 115) onto East Elm St. until you see the small parking lot on your right before the bridge.* The river is still a good place to fish, popular with the locals.

When you're ready to head north again, return to Main St. which leads to rte. 1. You can pick up I-95 from rte. 1, but we recommend continuing north briefly on rte. 1 to some of Freeport's outlets that you'd miss on the interstate.

Newly redecorated and as popular as ever, THE MUDDY RUDDER, rte. 1, 207/846-3082, overlooks tidal water and sea grass. The menu runs from seafood to steak, with wonderful soups. Onion soup or crab bisque are good bets. *Continuing north on rte. 1, you'll see signs for the HARRASEEKET LOBSTER COMPANY on your right. Turn here and head to* ***South Freeport*** *for your last look at the coast. En route is Staples Point Rd., on the right, which will lead you to Winslow Park, operated by the town of Freeport.* This former coastal farm offers swimming at a small beach, picnicking, and camping. *Playground, rest rooms, small admission.*

After returning to South Freeport Rd., you will pass through open farmland, with cows and sheep grazing in the pastures. The quiet village of South Freeport consists of a collection of attractive colonial homes and a boatyard with chandlery, dock, and the HARRASEEKET LOBSTER CO., 207/865-4888 or 207/865-3535. This is a blue-jeans and deck-shoe restaurant, with picnic tables outside and a dining room where picture windows overlook the harbor.

In the summer there's a ferry that takes passengers across the harbor on a 20-minute trip to ***Bustins Island***. A real step back into the past, this small island has neither electricity nor telephones; you can walk its circumference in under an hour. For a schedule, check at the Chandlery, South Freeport Harbor. *Ferry charges a fee for passengers, bikes, and dogs. The island has no beaches, no taxi, no place to buy lunch — just a few picnic tables near the boat landing and several hundred residents who won't begrudge you your visit, if you don't leave trash behind or intrude on their privacy.*

South Freeport Rd., which runs to your right toward **Freeport**, is a pretty trip, though a little hilly for many bikers. There are lovely old homes and water views along here.

In town this road becomes South St. before running into Bow St. Turn left if you're anxious to start shopping at the outlet stores. Turn right to reach two idyllic parks, still untouched by commercialism.

Sidetrip: ***Mast Landing Audubon Sanctuary***. This 150-acre tract of woods, fields, and marshland has an extensive network of trails. Mast Landing is named for the towering mast pines found here in colonial days. "Pinus strobus" grew straight with no branches all the way up to its crown. These trees may well have been 500 to 1,000 years old when colonists cut them down for ship masts. *Look for the sanctuary signs on the left, about a mile east of rte. 1; free.*

> By the late 17th century, a single mast pine would bring £100, but the work involved getting these masts from the forest to port was incredible. Sometimes 90-100 oxen were needed to haul **just one tree**, so heavy were these logs.

Sidetrip: **Wolf Neck Woods**. *Continue another mile down the road toward the water until you see a sign for the park on your right. About two miles after you turn right, you'll find yourself in 200 acres of hemlocks, pines, and mixed woods along a rocky peninsula.* No matter how hot it may be, this is the coolest spot around, but you may need insect repellant. Of special interest is the osprey sanctuary on Googins Island, just east of the neck at the northern end of the park. Look for their nests in tall, dead pine trees. *Numerous trails (some with balancing beam bridges for kids), picnic spots; cross-country skiing in winter. Active interpretation program, including guided hikes; call 207/865-4465 for current activities. Fee.*

"Right Smart Fellow, That Mr. Bean."

Heading left on Bow St. toward the commercial center of Freeport, you'll end up on rte. 1, directly across from the main entrance of L. L. Bean's retail store. Open 24 hours a day every day of the year, this establishment draws two million shoppers a year and has become a magnet for other retailers. (In the past three years 125 new businesses, mostly catering to bargain hunters, have opened their doors here.) The Bean Store is a well-run ship and worth visiting; the best bargains are in the Factory Store on the second floor.

Until Leon L. Bean opened his retail store to augment the highly successful mail-order business (the giant complex of industrial buildings south of town), things were not going well for Freeport. In 1977, for instance, the population was smaller than it was in the late 1800s. Like so many New England towns, Freeport began as a shipbuilding center and later diversified into shoe-making and tourism, with enormous hotels and a trolley line.

Today another transformation has taken place, and this booming town now seems able to call its own tune. When McDonald's wanted to turn the 1855 William Gore House into one more fast-food franchise, the locals rallied to prevent the desecration of a noted landmark. What resulted from

Freeport's "Mac Attack" was a McDonald's furnished with Queen Anne tables and chairs and tiny Golden Arches outside. The restaurant is located at 155 Main St., corner of Mallet Dr. and Main St.

No one comes to Freeport just to dine, but there are several places where you can sit down and relax without dipping too deeply into your "mad" money. JAMESON TAVERN, 115 Main St., 207/865-4196, is an attractive, if somewhat expensive, old inn right next to L. L. Bean's. Another popular place to eat is OCEAN FARMS, 23 Main St., 207/865-3101. Newly enlarged, it offers seafood specialities, including locally smoked trout, scallops, and mussels.

No one had thought the quest for independence from Massachusetts would be stalled at the national level, but Maine statehood became an issue linked to the balance of free states vs. slave states, part of the Missouri Compromise. Finally, at Jameson's Tavern in Freeport, the act that made Maine a state was signed in March, 1820.

Further south on Main St., or rte. 1, is THE BLUE ONION, 207/865-9396, where the locals eat. Scallops wrapped in bacon, sauteed snails, homemade soup and chowder, lobster pie, steak "au poivre," and chicken Maximillian with fresh oranges, ginger, and tarragon may make you want to do something else besides shop.

I-95 is nearby to speed travelers home or on to other adventures elsewhere. While the inland sidetrips, described running south from Freeport, are not as rich in scenery or history as the coastal route, they are worth considering as breaks from the sameness of divided highway and the license-plate game.

Inland Sidetrips.

If you're coming from the north, you might want to take the inland sidetrips first, as they are described from north to south and often add flavor to whatever part of the coast you're visiting. Or if you've come from the south on the coastal route, you may be ready for a change of scenery:

• ***Bradbury Mountain***, west of Freeport, is a good place to start. *Take Exit 20 off I-95 in Freeport (Mallett Dr., if you're coming from the center of town), and head west. When you get to the stop sign, turn left again onto Pownal Rd. (there will be a small sign here directing you toward Bradbury Mountain.)*

This roller-coaster back road takes you through some pretty farmland for about five miles before putting you in the middle of a sleepy, crossroads town, ***Pownal Center***. *Turn right at the flashing light, driving past the church and town hall. After about a half mile, you will see the entrance to* ***Bradbury Mountain State Park*** *on the left*. The 480-foot bald summit can be reached by two easy trails leading from the picnic area. It is worth the hike, for the views of Casco Bay and the White Mountains, with the rolling farmland in-between, are stunning. *A well-developed park, with a softball field, play area, picnic tables, and camping nearby. In the winter, the favorite activities are cross-country skiing, snowmobiling, and looking for moose. Fee.*

The first farmers in this part of the country had their work cut out for them. Chickens did not thrive well here in colonial days; wolves devoured sheep and goats. Although blights and pests also hampered growing things, the colonists developed their own cures. One 17th century account complains that apple trees brought from Europe to Maine were assaulted by woodpeckers and the fruit by worms. The solution was to bore a hole in the trees, which the settlers supposedly then filled with rum — neither birds nor insects returned!

Returning to the flashing light in Pownal Center, turn left to get back to I-95 and Freeport.

• If you're looking for something to entertain the kids after shopping in Freeport, you might consider ***The Desert of Maine****. From Exit 19 of I-95, take Desert Rd. west for two miles* to reach this unusual natural phenomenon, now a commercial tourist attraction.

This spot was not always a desert. In fact, when William Tuttle bought his three hundred-acre farm here in 1797, he successfully raised potatoes and vegetables. It wasn't until he converted his land into pasture for grazing that things turned to sand. As cattle chewed the closely-cropped grass, they actually pulled out clumps of sod, uncovering a large deposit of sand left from the last Ice Age, some 8,000 years ago. The sand began to spread, eventually covering several acres, and engulfing 70-foot pine trees.

Rock hounds can study a variety of mineral deposits, including felspar, quartz, micas, garnets and hornblende. *Self-guided tours and nature trails, as well as narrated coach tours. The original 18th century barn has been turned into a farm museum. There is also the "Only Sand Museum in the World" and a gift shop. Fee. Picnic area, camp sites.*

Retrace your drive back to I-95.

• Summertime brings special sporting events to this area. Exit 6 of the Maine Turnpike opens early in May, as the ***Scarborough Downs*** racing season gets underway. This harness racing track is popular with tourists and locals alike. *Closes late September; admission. Restaurant.*

• Or you can watch the ***Maine Guides***, a professional minor-league baseball team, playing at their stadium in Old Orchard Beach. *Take Exit 5 of the Maine Turnpike to I-195 toward Old Orchard. Bear left onto rte. 5 and look for the Police Station on your left after about a mile. Turn left just before the Police complex, then turn right at the Guides sign. Fee parking, admission. Refreshments.*

• For a closer look at Maine's southernmost mountain, ***Mount Agamenticus***, take Exit 2, off the Maine Turnpike to Wells. *Turn right onto rte. 1, continue all the way through Ogunquit village to the flashing light one-quarter mile south of town (Agamenticus Rd.) Turn right here, passing CLAY HILL FARM INN, 207/646-2272, an elegant restaurant that appears in the middle of nowhere. Halibut generously stuffed with lobster, filet mignon, or scampi are good choices; the chocolate desserts are hard to pass up.*

Drive about four miles in all to the stop sign and turn right continuing another 1.6 miles to a paved road on your right that will lead you up the mountain. ***Bicyclists please note:*** *There are several steep* *hills on this route, so it is not recommended for biking unless you are in top shape and looking for a challenge.*

> The first white men in this area referred to the White Mountains as "the crystal hills."

Mount Agamenticus rises out of this isolated section of Maine — all by itself. Until recently this was a ski area complete with summit lodge and chairlifts. Now the main attraction is the magnificent view — the ocean to the east and the White Mountains in the distance to the west from the observation tower.

On almost any day during the fall there will be at least one birder recording hawk sightings in his record books. As many as 5,000 hawks of various species have been seen here in a single day. Mt. Agamenticus, called the "Big A" by locals, also attracts naturalists because it is the northern boundary for a number of botanical species, including the black birch, chestnut oak, flowering dogwood (the only known site in Maine), and the spleenwort.

> There is a curious legend about this mountain: "Saint Aspinquid," an Indian convert to Christianity, was said to have been buried here in 1682 with a ceremony that included sacrificing thousands of animals on the mountain's summit.

You can either retrace your steps to Ogunquit or head south to York, where there are several restaurants on rte. 1 before you get to I-95. *If you want to go south, keep straight (rather than turning left at the "V" toward Clay Hill Farm and Ogunquit). Going straight will eventually bring you to rte. 1.* The small, rustic-looking, brown bungalow straight ahead on the other side of rte. 1 is FLO'S STEAMED HOT DOGS. Franks with Flo's special hot sauce pack people into this tiny hole-in-the-wall all year, except in May when the owner heads south for vacation.

Just a short ways south on rte. 1 is THE CAPE NEDDICK INN AND GALLERY, 207/363-2899, a much more up-scale place to dine. Sculpture, paintings, and an ambitious menu have made this restaurant "au courant" with the in-crowd. Fish chowder here is excellent and there are tempting specials, like shrimp grilled with New Orleans-style jalapeno sauce, chateaubriand topped with stilton cheese, or chicken breast stuffed with mushrooms, boursin, and tarragon.

For a scenic route south, follow the directions to rte. 1, but turn right onto Chase's Pond Rd., just before the bridge over I-95. This road passes the pond itself and, after three miles, a huge boulder on the right (a memorial to the 300 settlers captured or murdered in the York Massacre). Eventually, you'll return to the interstate just south of the York tollbooth.

Before the Indians attacked York in 1692, they are said to have piled their snowshoes against a boulder along Chase's Pond Rd., dubbed by locals as Snowshoe Rock.

• The York and Piscataqua Rivers and their tributaries led early settlers inland in this area; today there remain pretty back roads that still capture the rural flavor of northern New England. If you're looking for a change of scenery, try a lovely inland loop from York to ***South Berwick*** and back to I-95 at the Kittery Outlet Malls.

Until 1760 the boundaries of York County, Maine extended from New Hampshire to Nova Scotia.

From the Maine Turnpike in York, head south on rte. 1 for half a mile to rte. 91. Turn right here, and you will soon be in a peaceful inland part of the seacoast region known mostly to locals. This hilly, curving road promises something different around every turn, including pleasant homes (many of them quite old), family burial grounds, nurseries, greenhouses, herb farms, and tranquil views of the marshes and inlets of the York River.

Two and a half miles down the road, shortly after passing SCOTLAND BRIDGE INN, 207/363-4432, you will come to the McIntyre Garrison, pri-

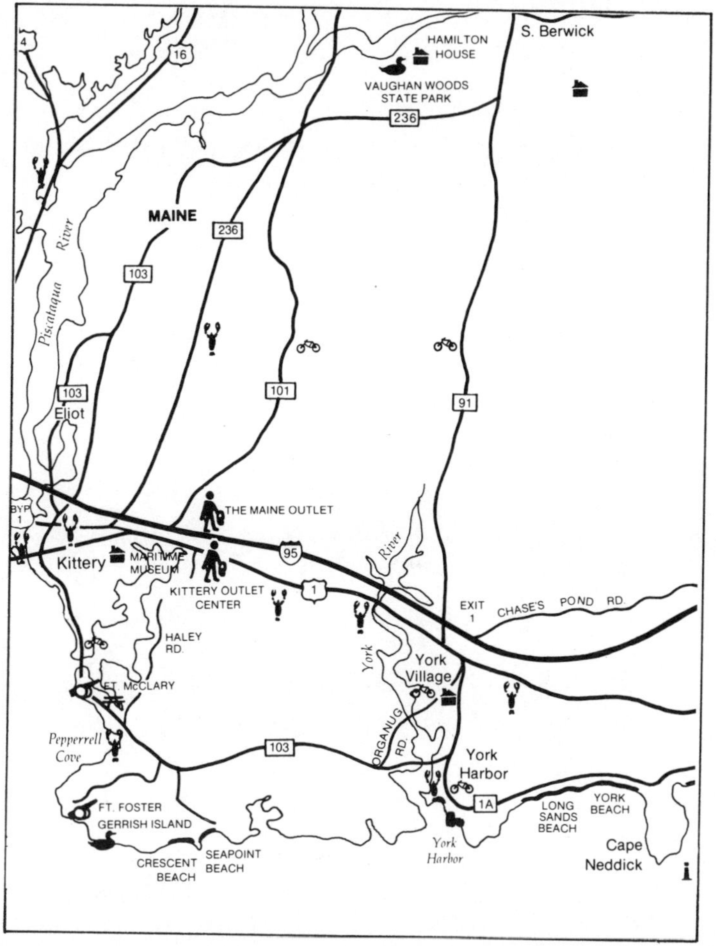

vately owned, on the left. Strategically sited on a hill overlooking the river, this fortified structure (built in 1640) is reputedly the oldest garrison in Maine. For security there is only one door, facing the river, rather than the road, and the log walls are almost eight inches thick.

This part of York is known as ***Scotland***, because so many of the settlers came from that country. Prisoners from the 1650 Battle of Dunbar, these Scotsmen were sent to the colonies by Oliver Cromwell and were allowed their freedom after serving their terms as bondsmen.

A prisoner's life in the colonies was not very different from a slave's, except prisoners might one day be free. Scotsman Alexander Maxwell received thirty lashes "upon his bareskin" for not behaving as his master would have liked; he was also threatened with resale in Virginia or Barbados. Nevertheless, he gained his freedom and was able to purchase 70 acres on the York frontier. In 1660 former fellow-prisoners Daniel Dill, two James Grants, and John Carmichael joined him here. As more Scotsmen followed, they built their own garrison and fought along with other York settlers against numerous Indian attacks.

Continuing west on 91, the landscape changes to pine woods, where few houses are visible from the road. *About 5.5 miles from the McIntyre Garrison is the intersection of rte. 236. Turn right here for a visit to the town of* ***South Berwick,*** *which boasts "the First Water Power Site in America."*

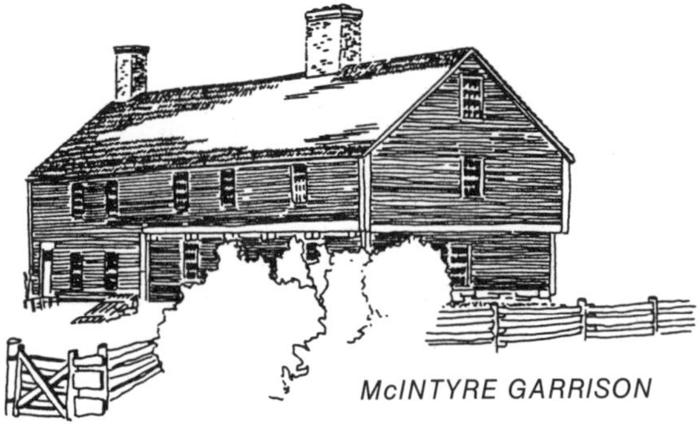

McINTYRE GARRISON

As early as 1640, there was a sawmill on the banks of the Salmon Falls River. In the forests nearby grew many tall, straight pines, coveted by the British Navy for their use as ship masts. The town developed with the expansion of the mill. Today, South Berwick is hometown to many of the workers at the Portsmouth Navy Yard, but it still retains its rural flavor.

Oxen dragged masts from the forest to the rivers, where they were floated downstream and kept in harbors like that at Portsmouth until the mast ships arrived from England.

The center of town consists of a small collection of stores mixed in with colonial and Victorian houses. The most notable building in town is the "dear old house and home" of author Sarah Orne Jewett. Her work includes a Revolutionary War romance, THE TORY LOVER, and a collection of stories about this area, THE COUNTRY OF THE POINTED FIRS. Of interest in the 1774 ***Jewett House*** are original and reproduction wallpapers, as well as paneling and period furnishings. The author's study (also her bedroom) is much the way she left it. *Open June 1-October 15, Tues., Thurs., Sat., Sun. Noon-5. The house is directly ahead of you as you enter the center of town on rte. 236.* 207/384-2454.

> "Because an old-fashioned town . . . grows so slowly and with such extreme deliberation, is the very reason it seems to have such a delightful completeness when it has entered fairly upon its maturity . . . The towns which are built in a hurry can be left in a hurry." Sarah Orne Jewett, 1884.

Head west on rte. 4 to the bridge which crosses the Salmon Falls River into New Hampshire. Just before the bridge, turn left at the brick power plant onto Liberty St. After passing a few pretty colonial houses, you will come to a stop sign. Turn right here, onto a quiet country road, offering fine views of the Great Works River on the left and the Salmon Falls River on the right. At the next stop sign, turn right onto Oldfields Rd.

Directly ahead will be the entrance to ***Hamilton House***, the grand Georgian mansion built in 1785 by wealthy merchant, Col. Jonathan Hamilton. From here he could overlook his busy shipyard, warehouses, and wharves along the river. The house, which has been restored to a simpler Colonial facade, was the setting for Sarah Orne Jewett's THE TORY LOVER. Inside, the house is furnished in a pleasing blend of city and country elegance. Also of interest is an impressive doll collection. *Open June 1-October 15, Tues., Thurs., Sat., Sun. Noon-5. Admission; 207/384-5269.*

Just past Hamilton House on Oldfields Rd. is a small gem of a park: ***Vaughan Woods***. Nearly six miles of secluded trails will take you through the 250 acres of hemlocks along the Salmon Falls River. Sometimes the silence is broken by the call of a pileated woodpecker.

A number of tree species are at the northern edge of their range here. Look the the shagbark hickory, whose long vertical strips of bark pull away from the trunk at both ends, and the black birch, whose wintergreen-smelling twigs were fermented to make birch beer. You may also find partridge berries in the carpet of pine needles on the forest floor. *Free. Picnic area; cross-country skiing.*

Continue south on Oldfields Rd. for about three miles, passing through the rolling countryside of South Berwick and ***Eliot***, *until you come to rte. 101. Turn left, continue across rte. 236, and after about seven lovely country miles through Eliot, you* *will end up at the stoplight at rte. 1 next to the Kittery Trading Post.*

> The most beautiful and versatile of all the Portsmouth clippers was built, without regard to cost, by Samuel Hanscom, Jr. of Eliot. With a figurehead of namesake Jenny Lind, Hanscom's "Nightingale" charged $100 to $125 to passengers she carried to the World's Fair.

Established in 1926, this is the anchor store of the mile-long Kittery outlet strip. While some of the other stores may be considered trendy, the Trading Post sells equipment to hunters, fishermen, and campers. If you are the outdoorsy type, and not impressed by the latest fads, this cavernous store is worth visiting. About a half mile south of here is the Maine State Liquor Store, a good place to stock up on your victuals, for the prices are usually 5 to 15 cents less than New Hampshire's. This is the only store in Maine that offers liquor at a discount. *Alternate route: For a quick route to I-95 and Kittery (ten minutes), turn right onto rte. 236 instead of continuing across it to 101.*

• For tax-free outlet shopping, visit Artisan Outlet Village, off rte. 1 (Lafayette Rd.), in Portsmouth. There are about a dozen stores in this small mall. *Take Exit 5 off the New Hampshire Turnpike to the traffic circle. Take the second spoke to the rte. 1 by-pass, which turns into rte. 1. After about two miles, turn right onto Mirona Rd., just past McDonald's; Artisan Outlet Village will be on the left, a half mile down the road. To reach the* ***Urban Forestry Center*** *(see page 15), continue south on rte. 1 to the stoplight at YOKEN'S restaurant (see page 22). Turn left onto Elwyn Rd., and the entrance will be on the left.*

• The North Hampton Factory Outlet Center is another small group of stores offering tax-free discounts. *Take Exit 2 off the New Hampshire Turnpike to rte. 101C, heading east toward Hampton; when you reach the stoplight at rte. 1, turn left. The stores are less than a mile on the right.*

• For a visit to historic ***Exeter***, one of New Hampshire's four original towns, *take Exit 2 off the New Hampshire Turnpike (I-95) and head inland on rte. 51. The best route requires getting off rte. 51 after a mile and a half onto rte. 101D. (Don't be misled by the exit sign which says Hampton and Rye — but not Exeter. This IS the most interesting route, even if it seems a little convoluted at first.) At the bottom of the exit ramp turn left, which will take you to 101C for three short and pretty miles to Exeter.*

As you approach the town, the road turns into High St., a comfortably shaded residential area with many lovely old homes. After crossing the bridge over the Squamscott River in the center of town, look for a parking space (no meters) and explore on foot. Just beyond the bandstand, the site of summer concerts, is the brick courthouse, with the Exeter Area Chamber of Commerce office entrance at street level. Those interested in detailed history may want to purchase, for a modest sum, a booklet of walking tours of Exeter. There are four tours covering a total of nine miles and 189 stops. After taking these very comprehensive tours, you will know more about Exeter's history than most natives do. *603/772-2411.*

Like many area rivers, the Squamscott has a 'fish ladder' to help salmon return to fresh water.

The town was founded in 1638 by the Rev. John Wheelwright, who originally settled in Boston, but was banished by the Massachusetts Bay Colony because of his liberal views on the separation of church and state. He and his followers moved to Strawbery Banke (Portsmouth), then up the Piscataqua River to Dover, and down the Squamscott River to what is now Exeter. The Wheelwright group made a deal with the Squamscott Indians, who gave the white men a large tract of land in exchange for allowing them to fish at the falls. (It doesn't seem like much of a deal, since the Indians had fished all they wanted and lived on the land quite comfortably before the good reverend arrived.) The actual treaty with Indian chief Wehanownowit's totem (mark) among the signatures can be seen at the ***Exeter Historical Society***, 111 Front St. In 1643, New Hampshire's settlers voted to become part of Massachusetts, but since Reverend Wheelwright was still considered ''persona non grata'' by that colony, he was forced to leave Exeter.

Prior to the Revolution, the town's fortunes rested with the Gilman brothers, who brought the first industry to the settlement, in the form of a sawmill at the falls. The ***Gilman Garrison*** still stands near the falls, at the corner of Clifford and Water Sts. An addition in 1772 disguises the facade of the garrison, but some of the original hand-hewn beams can be seen on the inside. *Open seasonally; admission. 603/227-3956.*

The town prospered in the 18th century as the shipbuilding and lumbering industries expanded. Squat gundalows plied the river, carrying supplies back and forth to the clipper ships docked in Portsmouth Harbor. Exeter became the seat of government for New Hampshire during the Revolution, since Portsmouth, full of loyalist-leaning Tories, was too vulnerable to attack from the sea.

The King's "broad arrow" policy caused the famous Mast Tree Riot of 1734 in Exeter. New Hampshire lumbermen "not troubled with nice scruples" managed to evade British claims to mast pines for years, until Surveyor General David Dunbar ordered his men to cut the King's arrow on lumber at a mill in Brentwood (part of Exeter). The locals, dressed up as Indians, roughed up Dunbar's men a little at Gilman's Tavern (now the Water St. parking lot), scuttled the inspectors' boats and destroyed their sails, making their retreat to Portsmouth an uncomfortable one.

Phillips Exeter today has about 1,000 students, male and female, and close to 40% receive financial aid. Its graduates include Daniel Webster, Robert Lincoln (son of President Abraham Lincoln), historian Arthur M. Schlesinger, and CONNOISSEUR editor Thomas Hoving.

At about this time, a wealthy merchant by the name of John Phillips founded ***Phillips Exeter Academy***, one of the country's premier prep schools. Front St., which goes up the hill behind

John Knowles' novel, A SEPARATE PEACE, describes a preparatory school that sounds amazingly similar to Exeter: "I walked along Gilman Street, the best street in town. The houses were as handsome and as unusual as I remembered. Clever modernizations of old Colonial manses, extensions in Victorian wood, capacious Greek Revival temples line the street, as impressive and just as forbidding as ever. . . . Like all old, good schools, [it] did not stand isolated behind walls and gates but emerged naturally from the town which had produced it . . ."

the bandstand, will take you through the heart of its beautiful elm-shaded campus. Much of the town's activity revolves around the Academy. THE EXETER INN, 90 Front St., 603/772-5901, remains steeped in "school-tie" charm and offers food, drink, and lodging. While the mills and wharves are long gone, Exeter is still a prosperous community, with light manufacturing and service businesses the dominant industries.

After exploring the town and campus, continue west on Water St. (in front of the bandstand) to Swasey Parkway, on the right. This peaceful, willow-shaded park along the Squamscott River affords views of Exeter's quintessential New England skyline. *To return to I-95, retrace your steps back to 101C and follow the signs to the turnpike.*

Designed by the Olmsted Brothers of Brookline, Massachusetts, the Swasey Parkway was built in 1929 over the Exeter town dump.

Sidetrip: ***Hampton Falls***. *For a more scenic route in the same direction as the turnpike, turn right off of 101C onto rte. 88, shortly after leaving Exeter.* This road passes through rolling farmland and acres of apple orchards before ending at rte. 1 in Hampton Falls, four miles to the south. The buildings you see along rte. 88 are a mixture of large new dwellings, colonial farmhouses, and impressive estates.

In 1981 gypsy moth caterpillars were so numerous that they stopped trains to Exeter on their tracks.

As you near Hampton Falls, look for Applecrest Farm, on the left. In the summer it's a farmstand, offering a wide variety of locally-grown produce. The rest of the year they sell baked goods, their own jams, fresh eggs, and a large selection of products made from the half dozen varieties of apples grown on the surrounding hills. In the winter they rent cross-country skis for exploring the extensive trail network which runs through the orchards.

After crossing over the New Hampshire Turnpike, one of the few signs of modern civilization on this route, you will pass an old burying ground on the right, and a pretty church on the left. Look at the clock and you will see something unusual about it. We'll leave this for you to discover. The Governor Weare House (1725) is also on the left, built by the first governor of New Hampshire.

When you reach rte. 1, you will be facing the Hampton Falls Shoppers Village, an attractive collection of about a dozen boutiques and food shops. Just to the north is the Hayloft, where many locals do their clothes buying. *Head left onto rte. 1 toward Hampton and the beaches, as well as Exit 2 of the New Hampshire Turnpike; or turn right toward Seabrook and Exit 1 of the turnpike.*

If you take rte. 1 north, you'll pass an enormous antique center on the right, Gargoyles and Griffins. Whether you're in the market for a 1930s Rolls Royce or a vintage Oriental rug, this showroom has it all: stained glass in every imaginable size and color, a pulpit or a mirrored bar, carousel horses, old toys and pinball machines. Further along rte. 1, you'll pass THE WIDOW FLETCHER'S TAVERN, 401 Lafayette Rd., 603/926-8800, possibly your last opportunity to indulge in seacoast dining (their chowder is an award winner).

Sidetrip: ***Newfields***. If Exeter makes you want to see a little more of picturesque inland New Hampshire, take the Swasey Parkway west of town. This narrow up-and-down road has no shoulders, but is lightly traveled. Skirting the placid Squamscott River, it passes through a mixture of pleasing landscapes — past pretty old colonials, stone walls, and tiny graveyards before reaching the town, four miles to the north. The handsome village of Newfields was part of Exeter until 1727, and later part of Newmarket, its northern neighbor, until 1849. The center of town consists of a general store with two gas pumps out front, the town hall (closed except for one evening a week for selectmen's meeting), a church, a small park with a liberty bell in it, and many attractive houses.

Continue north on rte. 85 for another half-mile to rte. 108. If it's dinnertime, turn left and in a half-mile you'll come to THE HALF BARN on the right, 603/778-7898, an attractive restaurant filled with antiques, quilts, and memorabilia. *Or turn right toward* ***Stratham*** *(pronounced* ***Strat****-ham)* **Circle** for another excellent dining opportunity and barns full of antiques and crafts for sale. One fine collection of Americana is the Collector's Eye, *located on the left, just after the merge with rte. 101;* another is The Antique Emporium, just east on rte. 101, heading toward Portsmouth. Next door is THE CARRIAGE STALL, 603/772-2138, where you can get a Bloody Mary garnished with cocktail shrimp, as well as quiches, salads, and sandwiches on homemade bread.

To reach the New Hampshire Turnpike and Portsmouth, continue east on 101 for another seven miles, speeding past the farms and meadows of Stratham and Greenland. On the way, you will pass **Stratham Hill Park** with its fire tower on the top, affording fine views of the countryside. The public is permitted to climb the tower, but be warned that it is steep and should not be attempted unless you are in good shape.

From here you can see a fair distance. But whether you're looking at New Hampshire or Maine, this coast is worth visiting — again and again.

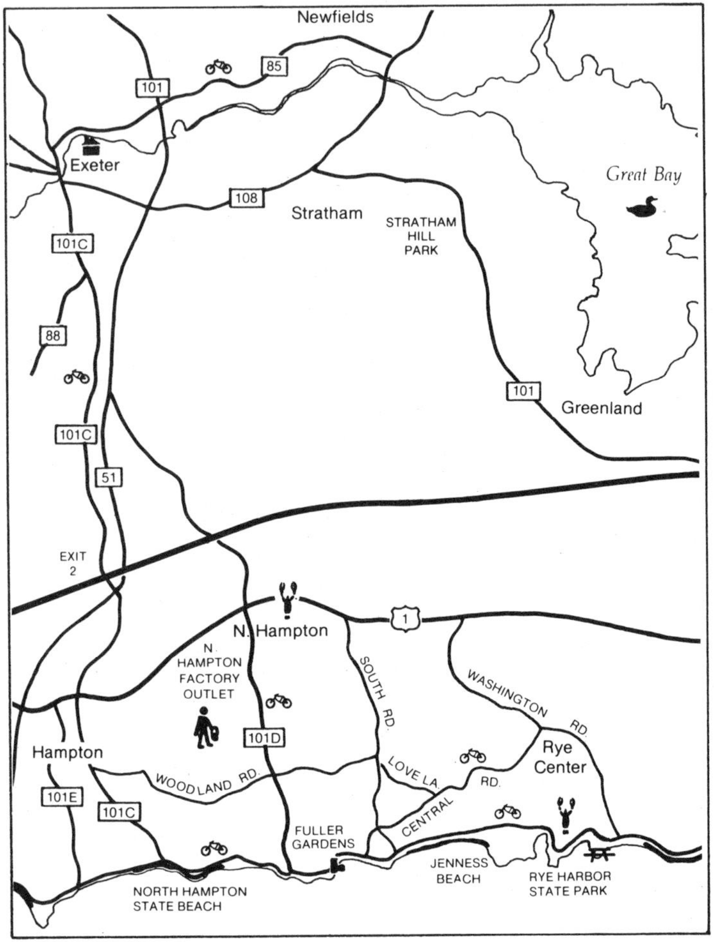

Index

NOTES

NOTES

NOTES

NOTES

NOTES